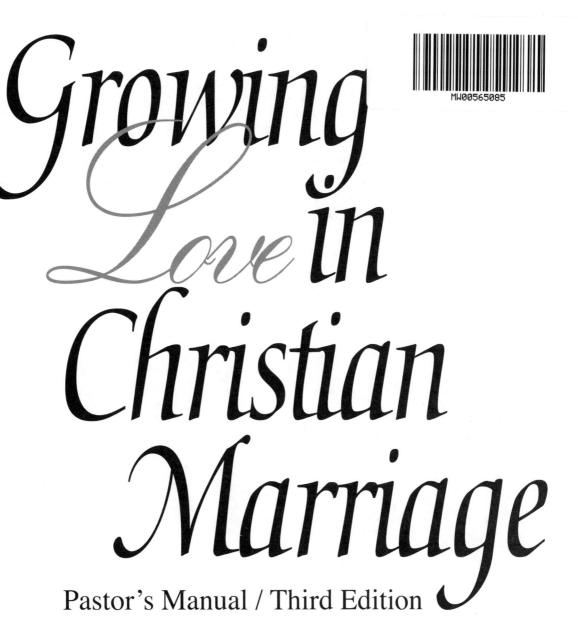

Growing Love in Christian Marriage

Pastor's Manual / Third Edition

JANE P. and S. CLIFTON IVES

Abingdon Press / Nashville

GROWING LOVE IN CHRISTIAN MARRIAGE
Pastor's Manual / Third Edition
Copyright © 2013 by Abingdon Press

This book is printed on acid-free, elemental chlorine-free paper.

ISBN: 978-1-4267-5791-4

13 14 15 16 17 18 19 20 — 10 9 8 7 6 5 4 3 2 1
MANUFACTURED IN THE UNITED STATES OF AMERICA

CONTENTS

PART TWO: WORKING WITH COUPLES

ACKNOWLEDGMENTS

We first met Leon and Antoinette Smith, authors of the 1981 edition of this manual, when they came to Maine to lead a Marriage Enrichment Training Event in 1974. They opened new doors for us in our relationship and helped us to grow both individually and as a couple. We are eternally grateful!

Leon and Antoinette are both clinical members of the American Association of Marriage and Family Therapists and are licensed in that field. Antoinette holds both an M.A. and an Ed.S. degree in Human Development Counseling and certification as a Sex Educator by the American Association of Sex Educators, Counselors, and Therapists (AASECT). Leon holds graduate degrees from Emory, Drew, and Columbia Universities, including a doctorate in Marriage and Family Living, and is certified as a Sex Therapist by AASECT. In addition to their co-therapy practice of many years, Leon and Antoinette have shared a vision of ministry to married couples that challenges and inspires us.

The Smiths' involvement with marriage enrichment began in 1951, when Leon, as pastor of Roswell United Methodist Church in Georgia, developed programs to meet the needs of a group of young expectant couples. As word spread, the Smiths were invited to lead workshops for other churches in the Atlanta area. Leon was also invited by The United Methodist Church to lead three-day marriage counseling workshops for pastors around the country.

In 1962, the Smiths moved to Nashville to work with the United Methodist national staff in the development of programs to strengthen marriages. The Smiths also worked closely with David and Vera Mace in the design and implementation of a leadership training program for the Association of Couples in Marriage Enrichment and continued training couples to lead Marriage Communication Labs until health issues forced them to retire. In the words of their son Mark, "They had a mission to help others—no matter who they were." Their 1981 edition of the Pastor's Manual for GROWING LOVE IN CHRISTIAN MARRIAGE has provided a valuable tool for church leaders seeking to minister effectively with engaged and newlywed couples. We feel honored by the invitation to update the Smiths' material and by their encouragement for us to do so.

We are grateful to Richard and Joan Hunt for their commitment to the revision and updating of GROWING LOVE IN CHRISTIAN MARRIAGE and for their good work on the Couple's Manual. Richard is Senior Professor of Psychology at the School of Psychology of Fuller Theological Seminary. An ordained elder in the Central Texas Annual Conference, he is also a licensed psychologist in California and has been a clinical member and supervisor in the American Association of Marriage and Family Therapy, Diplomat with the American Board of Professional Psychology, and Fellow in the American Association of Pastoral Counseling. Joan has taught in elementary and special education classes in public schools in Texas. The Hunts, long-standing members of the Association for Couples in Marriage Enrichment, have led marriage enrichment events at colleges, local churches, annual conferences, prisons, retreat centers, and in other settings.

We offer special thanks to Rod and Charlene Giles and John and Paula McKay for providing material for the chapter on mentor couples programs. Charlene, Director of Marriage and Support Ministries at Asbury United Methodist Church in Tulsa, Oklahoma, is a licensed marital and family therapist and a certified family life educator with a master's degree in counseling. Rod has advanced degrees in business and health administration and works as a planner in the area of senior services and housing. Charlene and Rod serve as directors of the Couple-to-Couple ministry at Asbury.

The McKays also participate in the Couple-to-Couple ministry and have served terms as training and referrals coordinators. John has a master's degree in International Management and is Senior Vice-president of a marketing research and strategy consulting firm. Paula, with a bachelor's degree in Journalism and History, works as Special Events Coordinator for the Tulsa City-County Library System.

We also wish to thank two pastoral counselors who loaned us resources and read our manuscript, making helpful suggestions we believe greatly improved the final product. The Reverend David C. Johnson, D.Min., Director of Pastoral Care and Education at Cabell Huntington Hospital, in Huntington, West Virginia, provides administrative oversight of pastoral care within the hospital, the pastoral counseling center, and the clinical pastoral education program. David is also clinically active as a pastoral counselor with a specialty in marriage, co-dependent relationships, and addiction recovery.

The Reverend Sky Kershner, D.Min., is Clinical Director of the Kanawha Pastoral Counseling Center in Charleston, West Virginia. An Approved Supervisor in the American Association of Marriage and Family Therapy and a Fellow in the American Association of Pastoral Counseling, his practice focuses primarily on individuals and couples in crisis and transition.

We want to thank several West Virginia United Methodist pastors who also shared with us ideas for updating this resource; the Reverend J.F. Lacaria, Associate Director of the West Virginia Council on Ministries; the Reverends Keith and Ruth Simmons; and the Reverend Patty Beagle.

Finally, we thank God for leaders in the marriage enrichment movement, both within the church and in the larger community, who through careful research and study have brought to this field new insights and many wonderful new resources. May others be blessed by these gifts as we have been blessed!

Cliff and Jane Ives
2001

INTRODUCTION

"It is by God's mercy that we are engaged in this ministry" (2 Corinthians 4:1).

The phone rings. You hear the excitement in Peggy's voice as she announces her engagement to Phil and asks you to perform their wedding ceremony. You check your calendar and make an appointment to meet with them, smiling as you recall the pleasure of watching their romance bloom and grow during their years of participation in youth fellowship activities.

Or perhaps the call is from an older couple. You may already know the bride-to-be, but not the groom, or vice versa. Or both may be strangers, distantly related to someone in your congregation or primarily interested in your beautiful sanctuary as a setting for their wedding. Perhaps this is a second marriage for one or both. In any case, the invitation to officiate at a wedding arouses anticipation and concern.

What Marriage Can Be

Marriage can serve as a channel for God's love and a means for realizing God's will for life here on earth. When two persons nurture each other's growth in an intimate, vital relationship, they reap benefits in the areas of health, wealth, sexual satisfaction, and personal happiness.[1] When couples affirm and support each other, sharing a forgiving and sacrificial love, everyone benefits—their children and extended families, their communities, and the world.

Growing up in the context of a satisfying marriage, children learn how to communicate effectively and how to make decisions and solve problems cooperatively. Watching their parents enjoy the pleasures and rewards of marriage, even while coping with its inevitable tensions, children develop realistic expectations for their own marriages and family life. Unfortunately, as marital failure and divorce increase in our society, more and more children lack a positive experience of marriage during their formative years.

The Breakdown of Our Marriage Culture

A 1999 National Marriage Project Report pointed out that "Americans have become less likely to marry. When they do marry their marriages are less happy. And married couples face a high likelihood of divorce. . . . Unmarried cohabitation and unwed births have grown enormously, and so has the percentage of children who grow up in fragile families."[2] Among the disastrous effects on children of this breakdown of family life are low self-esteem, psychological distress, poor social integration, problems with interpersonal relationships, educational failure, and lower socioeconomic levels.[3] Contrary to popular belief, divorce is not an event that persons get over in time; it is an ongoing reality with continuing negative consequences for those involved.[4]

You personally know couples who merely coexist or who lead separate, parallel lives. You also know couples who frequently display anger and hostility toward each other. Perhaps you have counseled with some of them or encouraged them to participate in a marriage-healing ministry. You most likely have dealt with children of divorce and know their ongoing struggles to move beyond the pain of their family's breakdown. Effective marriage preparation can help an engaged couple develop a realistic and covenantal understanding of marriage while learning concepts and skills that can make the difference between a fulfilling relationship and an unhappy one. This responsibility weighs heavily upon you, and you want to bring to your marriage preparation ministry the best possible resources. You do not want your church to be like those Michael McManus calls "blessing machines" because, while they help couples prepare for elaborate weddings, they do little to assist them in building lasting marriages.[5]

How Churches Can Help

Recent studies indicate that the keys to a happy marriage are a deep friendship between husband and wife and effective skills for communication and conflict management.[6] This is good news, because friendship can be nurtured and skills can be learned! By accessing current research-based information and by offering programs based on knowledge about what works, you can help engaged couples understand the challenges that lie ahead and learn how to achieve the kind of relationship they desire.

In addition to premarital counseling (Chapters 4, 5, and 6), you might offer a mentor couples program (Chapter 8) and/or organize group sessions for engaged and newlywed couples (Chapter 9). You can use a premarital inventory, such as that in the GROWING LOVE IN CHRISTIAN MARRIAGE Couple's Manual, to assess and build on the strengths couples bring to their marriage. Such instruments also surface areas of potential conflict, helping couples make informed decisions about their compatibility and begin to work through their differences.[7] You will want to provide opportunities for couples to continue marital growth after the wedding (Chapter 7) and shape the life of your congregation so that it nurtures and supports all marriages and families (Chapter 10).

As you work to strengthen marriages and families, we think you will find a stronger sense of community emerging in your congregation. The same communication and conflict-management skills essential to healthy marriages improve other relationships as well. The healing of family relationships, moreover, can free persons from energy-draining dynamics and empower them for ministry in the world.

An Overview of This Manual

The first section of this manual explores theological and theoretical issues related to pastoral counseling and marriage preparation in general. The second section provides specific suggestions and guidelines for working with engaged and newlywed couples, for effective use of the GROWING LOVE IN CHRISTIAN MARRIAGE Couple's Manual, and for establishing a larger framework of support and nurture for all marriages.

You will want to share much of this material with other church leaders and recruit a marriage and family ministries team to plan and implement whatever programs seem most appropriate. (See "Marriage and Family Ministries Team") Your marriage and family ministries team should study Chapter 10 on "Comprehensive Marriage and Family Ministries" and Chapter 2, "Theological Perspectives." After setting your priorities, focus in on the other chapters accordingly. The annotated list of resources included in this manual will help you select and access other materials and programs to enhance your marriage preparation work and to build a comprehensive marriage ministry for your congregation or parish. Websites listed under United Methodist Marriage and Family Ministries in the Resources section will be particularly helpful, as they provide supplementary resources designed specifically for use with GROWING LOVE IN CHRISTIAN MARRIAGE. Materials in other languages besides English may be found in the Resources section.

The first Guide/Checklist in Appendix IV at the back of this manual details steps for building a strong marriage ministry program. You may duplicate the second Guide/Checklist for planning and keeping track of your premarital work with individual couples. At the end of the manual, you will find an evaluation form you can copy or modify to solicit feedback from participants in your marriage preparation ministry.

We hope you will find this manual inspiring and useful as you and your marriage and family ministries team develop your own approach for nurturing healthy, enduring marriages in your congregation or parish.

PART ONE

THE MINISTRY OF MARRIAGE PREPARATION

"Through the testing of this ministry you glorify God by your obedience to the confession of the gospel of Christ and by the generosity of your sharing" (2 Corinthians 9:13).

1

THE PASTOR'S ROLE

"I came that they may have life, and have it abundantly" (John 10:10b).

Pastors help people experience the abundant life Jesus promised by fostering their spiritual growth. This involves both proclaiming the good news of God's redeeming love and helping persons discern and fulfill God's will for their lives. In your marriage preparation ministry, you seek to help couples "form a bond that honors the uniqueness of each other while weaving a common future together with God."[1] Because you also uphold values and principles that you believe reflect God's purposes for humankind, you may sometimes find yourself in ambiguous situations. For example, when confronted with a decision about whether to marry a particular couple, you will need to balance concerns about their readiness for marriage with the desire to offer them the resources of the gospel and the church at this critical point in their lives.

The Pastor as Counselor

In general, pastors in the counseling role bring the gospel to persons through ministries of *guiding, healing, sustaining*, and *reconciling*. Marriage preparation may be considered primarily a ministry of *guiding*, because it not only provides education and instruction, but also helps persons make decisions and plan for their future in the most constructive manner possible. Pastors help engaged couples face realistically the many adjustments they will need to make (Chapter 3), and consider the implications of a Christian understanding of marriage (Chapter 2).

Marriage preparation may also involve the ministry of *healing*, helping individuals overcome hurt and brokenness in their lives in order to become whole persons. During your work with engaged couples, pain from previous relationships or from family of origin experiences may surface, allowing you the opportunity to affirm God's grace, support the healing process, and encourage more extensive counseling or follow-up as seems appropriate.

The pastoral-care function of *sustaining* involves supporting or strengthening persons to cope with situations or conditions that cannot be changed. An individual may need help accepting and adjusting to a handicap or limitation, his or her own or the partner's. One or both persons may need support through a brief period of uncertainty or in facing deeper fears.

The *reconciling* function of pastoral care involves helping couples face their conflicts and reconcile any broken aspects of their relationship with each other and with God. It is important not to gloss over any difficulties couples may be experiencing, but to face them realistically and with understanding love. A premarital inventory surfaces issues that a couple is likely to struggle with in the future. You may be able to help them deal with these issues during the engagement period. Although the readiness of couples to recognize and deal with differences varies greatly, you will at least want to acknowledge the inevitability of conflict in an intimate relationship.

Personally you need to be honest about the limits of your ability and training. For instance, when the need for extensive psychotherapy is indicated, you respond as a counseling pastor to the extent that you are able. But beyond that limit, you refer persons to a competent professional therapist. Such referrals do not discredit your unique gifts and your training, but do reflect a realistic understanding of your own expertise.

Expectations and Perceptions

Because you are a pastor, couples are likely to come to your marriage preparation sessions with certain preconceived expectations. They may look up to you with trust and confidence in your willingness and ability to help. Some may expect you to serve as an authority figure and tell them what they should do. Others will strongly resist any kind of help or advice. Because a minister is often regarded as the protector of the community's moral standards, some may expect you to be judgmental. For example, you might be the last one to learn about a premarital pregnancy, and some people may be reluctant to talk with you about their sexual feelings or experiences. Take a few moments to reflect on the following questions:

How do you want to be perceived by those who come to you for marriage preparation?

What messages do you send through your sermons, leadership style, and general behavior, and how do those messages shape people's expectations of you?

Most ministers conduct premarital counseling sessions in the church building, perhaps in the pastor's study or other comfortable room. In smaller churches, such sessions may be held in the parsonage. In addition to concerns for privacy, the pastor should consider what the setting symbolizes to the couple. Persons who conceive of God as loving and forgiving will respond positively to meeting in the church. Those who believe in God as a tyrannical judge are more likely to feel uncomfortable, at least initially or until firsthand experience with a warm, caring pastor changes his or her mind.

What messages does your counseling setting convey to those who come to talk with you?

What changes in seating arrangement or decor could create a more hospitable atmosphere?

Sometimes you will experience conflict between your pastoral and your administrative roles. For example, while counseling with a woman who works with your youth group, you may discover that she is already living with her fiance. How will this knowledge affect your feelings about her as a role model for the young people in your church? How can you address that concern without alienating her in the counseling relationship?

What messages do your administrative decisions and your leadership style convey about your beliefs and about God's redeeming love?

Christian Community

The church is a special kind of community—one that cares about what happens to persons and participates in their celebrations and in their crises. You can find within your congregation valuable resources for helping couples prepare for marriage. Invite those with expertise in counseling, teaching, and organizing to serve on your marriage and family ministries team. Couples with healthy, growing marriages can serve as mentor couples (Chapter 8).

Utilizing mentor couples and/or working with couples in group settings (Chapter 9) will help you provide more extensive marriage preparation than you can possibly offer in private counseling sessions. By using mentor couples and groups, you can more efficiently meet the requirements of a community marriage agreement. For example, a fifteen-hour requirement could be met by three hours of private sessions with you and twelve hours of group sessions or meetings with mentor couples.

With the help of committed laity, you can develop within your church or parish a comprehensive program of marriage ministry, including relationship education for children, youth, and young adults, special events and ongoing enrichment experiences for married couples, and interventions for those in crisis. Your church can also enhance its marriage and family ministries by sharing resources and working cooperatively with other congregations.

How does your congregation's life together affirm the sacredness of marriage and family life?

What opportunities for learning and improving relationship skills do you offer?

Do families in crisis just disappear due to feelings of shame and false pride, or are they able to admit their need for help?

How can you nurture in your church an accepting climate acknowledging that "all have sinned and fall short of the glory of God" (Romans 3:23) and that God's grace is sufficient (2 Corinthians 12:9)?

How do/can you offer spiritual and practical assistance for members of your congregation to grow toward God's purpose for them in their daily lives and relationships?

The Pastor-Couple Relationship

The relationship between a counseling pastor and an engaged couple focuses on preparing them for their marriage. Even if you already know either or both persons, the content of marriage preparation sessions is likely to be more intimate and personal than that of your other encounters with them. You will discuss private and confidential matters they may not have shared with anyone else. They need to be assured that these personal discussions will be limited to the counseling setting and will not be continued during social contacts or in other settings. At best there will be openness and honesty, a free sharing of concerns and problems, but there may be some matters they are not yet ready to discuss. You can help them overcome embarrassment and fear by demonstrating *care*, *respect*, *acceptance*, and *affirmation*.

If you truly *care* for the persons with whom you counsel, loving them in a Christ-like way, you will communicate warmth and concern. Unless they have been so severely hurt in other relationships that they feel the need to protect themselves, most persons respond positively to such love. They may proceed cautiously, however, testing your dependability and the genuineness of your concern, gradually becoming more open and willing to share.

You express *respect* in counseling situations by trusting persons to make their own decisions and helping them to discover their own inner resources. You allow them to move at their own pace, and you

do not threaten them by probing. You respect their privacy and go only as far as they are ready to move at the moment. You keep confidences, unless you become aware of a situation that is life-threatening or otherwise dangerous, in which case you inform them that you must share that information in whatever way seems appropriate.

Acceptance encourages people to reveal more of their inner selves, in which process they may gain more insight and self-awareness. When a couple experiences your acceptance of their relationship as it is, they may share more of their deeper feelings about it and so gain a better understanding of each other and of the dynamics between them. For this reason, you will listen not only to their words, but also to their hearts, trying to understand feelings that may be hidden behind their words. If you are sensitive enough to reflect these feelings accurately, the couples with whom you counsel are likely to feel that you really understand. Even if you do not accurately reflect their underlying feelings, your genuine desire to under stand and your efforts to clarify what you perceive can help couples feel accepted and understood. They may then be able to drop energy-consuming defenses and put more energy into personal and relationship growth.

Along with acceptance, the persons with whom you counsel need to experience *affirmation* from you. Instead of judging, condemning, or correcting individuals and couples, make every effort to appreciate each one as a child of God in the process of becoming, just as we appreciate and enjoy a sunset unfolding or a garden in its various stages of growth. Affirmation inspires and challenges us to become our best possible selves, to live up to our God-given potential, and to give of ourselves to others.

Trying to establish a pastor-couple relationship may have value even when a couple resists participating in premarital counseling. One pastor tells about a couple who made excuses and avoided meeting with him until he indicated that he would not perform the ceremony unless they did. Even then, in the two hours they reluctantly scheduled, little seemed to be accomplished. The woman entered into the discussion as best she could but appeared embarrassed by the man's refusal to comment other than answering yes or no to direct questions. Although the pastor wondered if he had made a mistake insisting on the meeting, two years later the husband contacted him and asked for help with a communication breakdown in their marriage. The pastor met with the couple weekly for several months, during which time the couple made considerable progress. Near the end of the last of these sessions, the husband laughingly recalled his reluctance to participate in the premarital session, commenting, "But you know, I don't think I would have called on you for this help if you hadn't insisted on seeing us before we married."

Premarital Counseling: Coaching and Problem Solving

Premarital counseling is the process of helping persons assess their readiness for marriage, make plans for their wedding and life together, and solve problems that may arise in regard to preparation for marriage. Usually such counseling takes place with an engaged couple, although sometimes one or the other may not be available, as when one of them is away because of military service or work-related travel, or when they live at a considerable distance from each other. Another exception may be a couple, not engaged, uncertain as to whether to marry and interested in evaluating their relationship; or an individual may approach you for help exploring such issues. Occasionally premarital counseling will include persons other than the couple. For example, parents may be more involved if the couple is very young or if there are special concerns, such as a premarital pregnancy.

Premarital counseling usually involves a mix of coaching and problem-solving counseling. Although it is important to understand the difference between the two, you need to be sensitive and flexible enough to shift easily from one mode to the other as needed.

Coaching

The coaching aspect of premarital counseling involves four steps. The first step is helping the couple *assess their readiness for marriage*. You may guide them in exploring their understanding of the nature of marriage, including theological concepts, as discussed in Chapter 2, and practical considerations, such as the normal stages of marriage and signals that a relationship is in danger, as discussed in Chapter 3. You may help them consider what they

bring to marriage as individuals, the adjustments they are already making with each other, and their plans for dealing with continuing adjustments (or developmental tasks) after marriage (Chapter 7). Your marriage preparation program should be rigorous enough to help couples with weak relationships realize that concern before the wedding.[2]

A second step is helping the couple *identify needs*, both their unique individual needs and those they experience as a couple. You also want to help them consider the changes they can anticipate in the years ahead. Couples may identify some of their needs rather easily through responding to questions, verbally or in writing, but you may also have in mind needs of which they may not be aware. For example, most couples need help learning to deal with conflict or adjusting to sexual changes over time. However, you will also know specific needs of couples with whom you have used the questionnaire in the Couple's Edition or some other premarital inventory. You and the couple should decide together which needs to work on in the premarital counseling sessions. Engaged couples may be so distracted by the complex details related to the wedding itself that you can focus only on those areas that seem urgent to them at the moment.

The third step in coaching is helping the couple *discover resources for addressing their needs*, those that have surfaced and those of which they are not yet aware. These resources may include books and other media, mentor couples, enrichment groups and events, and professional services. Some resources for continuing marriage growth are listed in the GROWING LOVE IN CHRISTIAN MARRIAGE Couple's Manual, which is, of course, a valuable resource itself. Others are listed in the back of this manual. You will also be aware of organizations and agencies in your own church and community that support couples in their ongoing marital journey. Skills for effective communication and conflict-management serve as resources, too. Coaching couples through the problem-solving steps in Section 4.3 of the Couple's Edition will help them experience and practice a process that they can actually use on their own.

The fourth step in coaching involves helping the couple *plan for their life together*. Encourage them to apply the insights, information, skills, and resources discovered in premarital counseling while making specific plans for the years ahead. You may find it necessary to point out certain information or principles that you think have significance for them and assist them in using these in their planning. For example, reading a chapter on money management may not give them enough help. You may need to review with them the items and amounts in their budget, if they are open to that, and help surface the emotional issues they bring to the area of money management.

Problem-Solving Counseling

Premarital counseling also offers the opportunity for the pastor and the couple to work together on mutually defined problems. In addition to resolving given problems, such work can increase the couple's confidence and skill for handling problems in the future. Problem-solving counseling occurs in the midst of coaching whenever an issue arises that one or both wish to pursue further. Or a person may seek out the pastor for counseling because of increasing awareness of a problem as the wedding date draws near. Effective problem-solving counseling requires *mutual agreement* on the nature of the problem. For example, a woman intent on getting the pastor's help to persuade her fiance to agree to a certain type of wedding will not be amenable to learning how to be less demanding and more open to other than her own point of view.

Another essential condition for problem-solving counseling is *mutual consideration*. Pastors show consideration by demonstrating genuine concern for persons, feeling with and for them regardless of what they may reveal. Judgment and condemnation usually cause defensiveness, but acceptance frees persons to take responsibility for what they do and who they become. Those receiving counseling show consideration by working within the limits of the counseling relationship, by not making unreasonable demands through numerous telephone calls or during chance encounters. They should consider the pastor a counselor who can help them make their own decisions, not someone who will take over their responsibility for themselves.

Confidentiality is essential if counseling is to reach any significant depth. A young man in his late twenties had been counseling with his pastor, trying to decide whether or not to become engaged to the woman he had been dating for several years. One day he mentioned this matter to the pastor's wife and was surprised to discover that she did not know anything about it. Assured that his pastor did honor confidentiality, he brought up concerns about his sexual orientation during his next counseling session. The pastor believes the young man would not have felt free to discuss this sensitive topic with him if the pastor's wife had known anything about their sessions.

On occasion, one or more sessions of premarital counseling may become family counseling in which the pastor meets jointly with the couple and some or all of the parents involved. In one situation, communication had completely broken down between a young couple and their parents, who objected to their children marrying so young. After meeting with the couple several times and then with both sets of parents separately, the pastor arranged for all six of them to meet together. He facilitated a process in which each person shared his or her feelings and point of view. Following that sharing, which led to increased understanding and openness, the pastor was able to help this family work out a mutually acceptable plan.

A pastor in the counseling role serves as a facilitator, providing the opportunity for something to happen and an atmosphere in which it is easy to share. You can offer guidance and train couples to use problem-solving strategies. You can give encouragement and support. You can make suggestions, affirming the couple's freedom to accept or reject them. You can point out certain facts and forces you think the couple is overlooking, but they must decide what to do with this information. In short, you help them make a self-determined resolution of their problem, but at no point do you take over their responsibility. You can trust God to work in their lives entirely apart from your efforts. Ideally, the resolution of a problem in premarital counseling is some form of mutually satisfying agreement between those counseled. That may mean accepting a difference and learning how to cope with it, but for some couples, the resolution may be a decision not to marry.

Beyond solving specific problems, however, it is even more important that couples be strengthened to work out their lives together. Counseling can help individuals gain sufficient ego strength, self-understanding, and courage to risk an openness with each other that they have not known before. Premarital counseling can also contribute to a person's growing sensitivity to the partner's needs and can stimulate a willingness to respond with sympathetic understanding and love. In facing their differences and tensions, a couple may begin to come to terms with their need for both intimacy and distance and start working toward some mutually satisfying balance. Hopefully they will discover that their marriage relationship cannot be taken for granted, but must be nourished and cultivated in order to grow.

Pastors must not allow themselves to be manipulated or controlled by those with whom they counsel. You may refer persons to a pastoral counselor, psychologist, or psychiatrist if they seem to need more specialized assistance than you are trained to give. Many pastors consult regularly with a pastoral counselor or psychotherapist about their counseling practices in order to be sure they are not missing important insights or getting in over their heads.

Decisions Regarding Particular Weddings

While working with a couple who comes to you for marriage preparation, you will naturally assess their readiness for marriage to be sure you feel comfortable marrying them. This is a matter of personal integrity and of responsibility to the church and community and the couple themselves. According to *The Book of Discipline of The United Methodist Church*, "The decision to perform a ceremony shall be the right and responsibility of the pastor."[3]

Without being judgmental, therefore, you will want to consider certain questions as you interview the couple. Some of the questions listed below relate to facts; others are more subjective. If you are uncertain about some of the answers, you might request more sessions or refer the couple to another professional, such as a pastoral counselor or psychotherapist, for additional help.

Screening Questions

1. *Are legal requirements being met in regard to the license, age or parental consent, and waiting period? Are your church's requirements being met?*
2. *Do these persons give sound reasons for wanting to get married?*
3. *Are they entering marriage freely or under duress?*

4. *Are they mature enough mentally and emotionally to understand the meaning of the vows and to give reasonable promise of fulfilling them?*
5. *Do they give indications that they intend to fulfill their marriage vows, or do they seem to take them too lightly?*
6. *Are there any serious mental, emotional, physical, or other handicaps that might endanger their marriage? Have these been adequately understood, accepted, and dealt with insofar as possible?*
7. *Is there such marked incompatibility of their personalities that psychological testing is indicated?*
8. *Are there differences in age, background, values, and so forth that may either enrich or threaten their marriage?*
9. *If this is a second marriage, has sufficient time elapsed since the death(s) or divorce(s) for the person(s) to have overcome the hurt and made adequate preparation for this new marriage?*
10. *Have they considered the impact of children on their marriage? Of blending families, if either or both already have children?*
11. *Is the couple willing to participate in adequate premarital preparation so that any questions can be addressed further and dealt with through the sessions?*

Hopefully you will be able to make a tentative assessment of a couple's readiness early in your work with them, but you will review this assessment as the interviews progress. By indicating early on that you want to evaluate your work together with them, you set the stage for sharing your perceptions. If you have real questions about the outcome of the marriage, these should be expressed. If you have built some level of trust with them, you can share your concerns nonjudgmentally, with a sense of genuine caring. Of course you are not responsible for making the decision for the couple to marry or not to marry. They always have the option of going to someone else, but you have the responsibility for deciding what you will or will not do.

Questions to Ask Yourself

1. *Can I in good conscience perform this ceremony? If not, will they marry anyway, and who will do it?*

2. *What effect would my refusal have on the couple's relationship to me? To the church?*
3. *What will the couple gain or lose, if I decide not to marry them?*
4. *If I decide to go ahead and marry them, in spite of my concerns, what will I be communicating to them? What will I be saying about myself? My theology? My role as pastor?*
5. *How will I provide ongoing care and support? Should I consider asking them to continue in counseling after the wedding?*

These are difficult questions. The primary guideline for your decision is your care for this couple and for their future. If they decide to marry even when you feel it may not work out well, you may choose to stay involved in order to provide pastoral support.

Your Personal Experiences and Attitudes

Whether married or single, you have your own unique experience with and attitudes toward marriage. Your beliefs about marriage have been shaped by your parents' relationship, your own relationships, and the marriages of other persons you know well. It is important to lift subconscious beliefs and attitudes to conscious awareness and to consider their validity and their impact on your work with engaged couples and newlyweds. If you are divorced, it is especially important that you work through your feelings in regard to that experience.

Get in Touch With Your Beliefs About Marriage

Set aside some time to journal and reflect on the following questions and/or invite colleagues to discuss them with you.

1. *How did your parents (and other significant role models) show their love and concern for each other? What do you think is essential for a happy, healthy marriage?*
2. *What did you feel was missing in your parents' marriage? How has this affected you and your attitude toward marriage?*
3. *To what extent is your approach to engaged and newlywed couples shaped by your own experi-*

ences? What other sources of information and understanding have influenced you? What other sources might be helpful?*

If you are married, your parishioners probably know your spouse and have some feelings about the quality of your marriage. Many persons have difficulty accepting that pastors are human and might have problems in their personal lives or in their marriages. The pressure on a pastor to demonstrate a happy marriage may cause some ministers to cover up problems and to resist seeking help when it is needed. Although a counseling pastor does not need to be perfect and does not need to have a perfect marriage, self-understanding and awareness of the dynamics of an intimate relationship are critical. Clergypersons who accept conflict as a natural part of a healthy and growing relationship present a realistic model to which other couples can relate and can guide couples from the authority of their own experience. Marital growth experiences, such as those listed in the Resources section, offer pastors opportunities not only to strengthen their own marriages, but also to gain knowledge and skills for more effective marriage preparation ministries. Some pastor-spouse couples who have received special training through marriage enrichment programs or through professional coursework offer marriage preparation as a team. Such couples can model and teach communication and conflict-management skills to individual couples or in group settings.

An Exercise for You and Your Spouse

Invite your spouse to spend an hour or so with you reflecting together on your marriage. Separately, each of you draw a circle, labeling it "My Inventory of Our Marriage." Divide your circle into four quadrants labeling them as follows, starting at the top left quadrant: "What I like most now," "What I like least now," "Past values and experiences now missing," and "Future values and experiences desired." Separately each of you fill in the four quadrants with as specific and honest responses as possible. After completing your circles, take a brief break and then share what you have written with each other.

As you listen, try to understand the other's statements without becoming defensive or judgmental. Try to accept feelings as they are, not counting them right or wrong and not attempting to change them. When each of you feels heard and understood (not necessarily agreed with), take turns responding to each other (not reacting). Rejoice in the strengths you have affirmed and express appreciation for whatever desires for change have been shared. Choose one of the changes on which you both can agree and plan how to implement it.[4]

2

THEOLOGICAL PERSPECTIVES

"Be subject to one another out of reverence for Christ" (Ephesians 5:21).

Christian marriage preparation takes place within a framework of Christian faith and specific understandings about God, humankind, and marriage itself. Faith, however, involves not just giving intellectual assent to a body of doctrine, but actually living in a faith relationship with God in the context of Christian community. When we live in faith, trusting God and responding to God's love as revealed in Jesus Christ, we open ourselves to expressing God's love through all our life experiences and relationships.

How do you define and describe Christian faith?

The Nature of God

Fundamental to Christian faith is our experience and understanding of the Triune God. The Holy Scriptures and the doctrines of our church define three different but related aspects of the nature of God: the Creator, the Redeemer, and the Sustainer.

As the Creator, God is ruler and maker of all things, all persons, and institutions, including marriage. Creation is not finished but continues in the present and into the future. God is the God of all life and is concerned about every aspect of life, including what we would consider most mundane. Nothing is outside God's love and care. God is also the God of all truth, providing insights through sociology, psychology, education, and other disciplines, as well as theology. We try to comprehend and make use of all knowledge that is compatible with our Christian faith.

When we speak of the Redeemer, we mean that God was in Christ, that Christ reveals God's nature, God's love, and God's will. The self-giving, victorious love of God is seen concretely in the life, death, and resurrection of Jesus. God, although revealed in many ways, is made known to us most clearly in Jesus Christ; therefore we call ourselves Christians and seek to realize the Christian quality of life in all our experiences, including marriage.

As the Sustainer, God continues to work in the lives of individuals, in families, and in other relationships, as well as through the church. We are not alone. God is with us amidst all the perplexities and problems of life. Through the Holy Spirit, God continues to give us direction and power to live in steadfast love and to do God's will in all things.

How do you understand and describe the nature of God?

Personal Responsibility and Christian Community

Each person must discern God's will for him- or herself in each particular circumstance using the best insights available from all sources. We need to beware of the temptation to mistake our own desires for God's will. We can best protect ourselves from this error by applying the quadrilateral based on John Wesley's teachings: Scripture, tradition, reason, and experience. This means that we thoughtfully weigh God's Word as it comes to us through the Scripture and through the traditions of the church, but we also consider the continuing revelation of the Holy Spirit through our personal experiences and through our ability to reason.

Christian community affords further protection by providing contexts for working out one's understanding of the will of God. However, an imperfect Christian community, made up of sinners as is always the case in this world, must not become a coercive structure attempting to control individuals. Each person must be free to respond to his or her understanding of the will of God, informed by Scripture, tradition, experience, and reason.

God's Purposes for Humankind

Certain fundamental Christian beliefs have special significance for marriage.

1. Human beings are creatures of God. Each one has worth and should be treated with dignity and respect. "Have we not all one father? Has not one God created us?" (Malachi 2:10a).

2. God created us female and male, of equal worth. Equality of both rights and responsibilities serves as the basis for mutuality in marriage. "So God created humankind in his image, in the image of God he created them; male and female he created them" (Genesis 1:27). Paul's admonition to wives in Ephesians 5:22-24 should not be taken out of the context of the preceding verse, "Be subject to one another out of reverence for Christ" (Ephesians 5:21)—nor of his ensuing words directed to husbands in verses 25 and 26.

3. Although we are influenced by factors in our background and circumstances, we are essentially free and responsible creatures. We may choose to obey God's will for us, or we may turn away from God in sin. "For you were called to freedom, brothers and sisters; only do not use your freedom as an opportunity for self-indulgence, but through love become slaves to one another" (Galatians 5:13).

4. In spite of our rebellion against God, we can through grace become aware of our condition, turn, respond to God, and receive the redemption offered in Jesus Christ. "So if anyone is in Christ, there is a new creation: everything old has passed away; see, everything has become new!" (2 Corinthians 5:17).

5. We are whole persons who must be understood in terms of all dimensions of our being: body, mind, and spirit. All are interrelated. Although we are motivated by certain physical, emotional, and social needs, most important of all is our search for meaning. We long to know what is good, true, and beautiful and to understand the significance of life in terms of ultimate values. "Happy are those who find wisdom, and those who get understanding" (Proverbs 3:13).

6. Human beings are dependent on God's providential care. Only in relationship with God can we truly know ourselves, overcome evil, and experience the abundant life God intends for us. "Know that the LORD is God. It is he that made us, and we are his; we are his people, and the sheep of his pasture" (Psalm 100:3).

7. Our mutual dependence on God makes us interdependent with others; we are social beings who cannot live in isolation from other people. Our full development as persons depends on wholesome relationships with others, including at least some intimate relationships in which we can be fully open and known. "This is my commandment, that you love one another as I have loved you. No one has greater love than this, to lay down one's life for one's friends" (John 15:12, 13).

8. Life is not fixed. Change is possible even though it may seem difficult or unlikely. Even where we experience painful past history and discouraging present conditions, God is at work in the lives of individuals and families to nurture growth and to restore broken relationships. "And the one who was seated on the throne said, 'See, I am making all things new'" (Revelation 21:5a).

9. Although the full reality of God's will for humankind may never be realized in our lifetime, Christians are called to acknowledge and demonstrate the reign of God in all areas of life. "He has told you, O mortal, what is good; and what does the LORD require of you but to do justice, and to love kindness, and to walk humbly with your God?" (Micah 6:8).

10. Our concerns and our hopes are not limited to this present world. We believe that life as we know it is but a part of something greater and that someday we will know the triumph of life over death and the ultimate victory of good over evil. "Now faith is the assurance of things hoped for, the conviction of things not seen" (Hebrews 11:1).

How would you add to or change the above statements of Christian belief?

God's Purposes for Marriage

Christians view marriage as a basic social structure given by God in creation. " 'For this reason a man shall leave his father and mother and be joined to his wife, and the two shall become one flesh.' So they are no longer two, but one flesh" (Mark 10:7, 8). This does not mean that God intends for every person to marry, nor that those who marry are thereby superior to single persons. Rather, we believe that God has some particular purposes for marriage and for those persons who choose to marry.

One purpose, or function, of marriage is *union*. When two people marry, they create a new unit, without, of course, losing their individual identities in the process. Ideally, persons of equal worth form an interdependent unit through which they find their individuality validated and strengthened. Sexual intercourse serves as a powerful symbol of and a means for nourishing this union, but marriage involves much more than physical coupling. It is a joining of two whole persons, a physical, mental, and spiritual joining that aids and stimulates each other's personal growth.

Another purpose of marriage is *fellowship*. In the second creation story, Genesis 2:18, God says, "It is not good that the man should be alone." We believe God instituted marriage as a means for overcoming loneliness and isolation. Husband and wife may complement and fulfill each other, but this does not mean that all of one's companionship needs can be met by one person. That would be expecting too much of marriage and put too great a burden on one person. We all need a larger community of family and friends, but the deeper intimacy and friendship of marriage is a special gift. Our church also affirms human sexuality as one of God's good gifts.[1] Mutually satisfying sexual expression strengthens and deepens the fellowship between husband and wife and nourishes their companionship.

A third purpose of marriage is *procreation*. Within marriage, Christians believe that God intends for new life to be conceived and children to be brought into the world. This does not mean that all couples must have children, nor that couples who choose not to have children are somehow inferior to those who do. It does mean that procreation within marriage is God's plan for continuing the population. Ecological awareness, however, suggests that God's instruction to "be fruitful and multiply" (Genesis 1:28) should be considered within the framework of personal and societal responsibility. In regard to procreation, each couple needs to discover the will of God for themselves at particular times and places, taking into account physical, emotional, economic, and social factors, as well as their own personal gifts and limitations.

A fourth purpose of marriage is *nurture*. Christians emphasize that to achieve full growth, adults and children need spiritual nurture, not just the meeting of physical, psychological, social, economic, and educational needs. Marriage provides the opportunity for husband and wife to help each other grow to their fullest potential that they may better serve others and contribute to making this world a better place. Those who decide to have children assume responsibility for nurturing them, with the assistance of their extended families, church, and community agencies as needed.

How would you describe the functions of marriage?

The Nature of Marriage

Marriage is meant to be a *monogamous, lifelong union based on love and fidelity*. Our marriage ritual expresses this intention in the words "forsaking all others, be faithful to her [or him] so long as you both shall live."[2] Marriage vows are meant to be honored not just as long as it is convenient and pleasing to do so, but for life. In fact, couples are reminded that difficulties are to be expected: "for better, for worse, for richer, for poorer, in sickness and in health."[3]

Love and fidelity are essential to each of the functions of marriage—union, fellowship, procreation, and nurture. The deep companionship of true marriage cannot grow in an unstable, temporary atmosphere, but only within a committed relationship. Furthermore, marriage needs to provide a durable and stable basis for bearing and rearing children. Infidelity, in its broadest sense, includes not just extramarital sexual involvement by one or both partners, but even the failure to give priority to the marriage and family relationship over work, recreation, family of origin, or other interests. Loyalty is made visible in the marriage partners' faithfulness to their marriage covenant and to each other and in their common commitment to protect their relationship from influences or dynamics that might damage or weaken it.

What qualities do you consider essential to the nature of marriage?

If marriage is intended to be a lifelong union, how then do we understand divorce?

Divorce and Remarriage

When asked about divorce, Jesus emphatically stated God's intention for marriage to be permanent: "Have you not read that the one who made them at the beginning "made them male and female. . . . For this reason a man shall leave his father and mother and be joined to his wife, and the two shall become one flesh'? So they are no longer two, but one flesh. Therefore what God has joined together, let no one separate." (Matthew 19:4-6. See also Mark 10:6-9.)

We recognize this statement as an expression of the ideal but not necessarily a binding decree on everyone. Jesus did not, in general, lay down legalistic requirements to be applied rigidly in every case. Insistence on the absolute indissolubility of marriage fails to recognize what might be necessary in exceptional cases. A marriage, like any other social relationship, must be evaluated in terms of what it does to the persons involved—all the persons, including the children. Therefore, in particular instances, separation or divorce may be the necessary solution when a marriage is destroying the persons involved. Before giving up on a relationship, couples should be sure that they have made every possible effort and accessed every available resource to bring healing and reconciliation.

God's forgiving love as we know it in Jesus Christ leads us to believe that a person is not forever doomed by a mistake, even one involving marriage. We believe, however, that remarriage after divorce (or after the death of a spouse, for that matter), should come only after enough time has passed for a person to overcome the hurt and adequately prepare for a new marriage. In view of the seriousness with which the Scriptures and the traditions of our church

regard divorce, we think a pastor should solemnize the marriage of a divorced person only when satisfied by careful counseling of the following:

- that the divorced person is sufficiently aware of the factors leading to the failure of the previous marriage;
- that the divorced person is sincerely preparing to make the proposed marriage truly Christian;
- that enough time has elapsed between the divorce and the contemplated marriage for adequate preparation and counseling. (See "Screening Questions" and "Questions to Ask Yourself" in Chapter One, The Pastor's Role.)

Do you agree with these guidelines? Would you change some? Would you add others?

Marriage as Vocation and Covenant

For the Christian, marriage and family life is a vocation, a calling. When Christians choose to marry, they do so responsibly, seeking to be faithful to God's will for them in this relationship, as in every other area of life. Mature Christians do not drift into marriage, but choose deliberately to marry in response to God's call. They do not allow themselves to be so overwhelmed by their feelings that they fail to consider carefully every aspect of their relationship—physical, emotional, social, economic, and religious.

Christian marriage is a covenant relationship under God, not merely a legal contract or social institution. In this covenant relationship, husbands and wives perform a mutual ministry of self-giving. They accept each other for better or for worse, and they enter into a new kind of "belonging" to each other. A Christian couple will continue in their marriage not simply because of the external pressures of society nor because of the level of internal personal satisfaction, but because they affirm marriage as a sacred covenant relationship. We do not mean by this that a man and woman are bound to maintain an empty form of marriage after all life and spirit have gone out of it. Rather, we expect a couple to work for the growth and enrichment of their relationship so that it continues to bless their lives and the lives of others within their sphere of influence.

The spirit does not go out of a marriage all at once. Rather, there may be a process of slow death based on a lack of positive interactions and an accumulation of negative experiences, with many danger signals along the way.[4] As a pastor, you can help couples see that they have an obligation to be alert to these danger signals and to react to them constructively. You can urge them to do their best to work out their inevitable difficulties with understanding and love, allowing the redemptive grace of God to work in their individual lives and in their relationship. You can also point them to opportunities for growth in marriage, offered by your local church or community, or available through the church at large and other organizations (see Chapter 10 and the Resources section).

The fact that husbands and wives are Christians does not make them perfect. As limited human creatures who need to grow in grace and love, they must permit God to continue to work in their lives and relationship. A Christian marriage is not one in which there are no problems, but one in which a couple tries to find constructive solutions to problems as they arise. Together, husband and wife need to cooperate fully with God in changing whatever causes difficulties in their lives and hinders the full expression of divine love through them. Indeed they may discover that some of their greatest growth comes through their problems and struggles. Harville Hendricks, in *Getting the Love You Want*, suggests that we choose mates who will help us grow according to a spiritual and emotional agenda of which we may not be consciously aware.[5] Because what attracts us often involves differences that cause conflict in intimate living, we may not recognize the opportunity to grow as a gift!

The Holy Spirit empowers husbands and wives to live patiently and generously with their marriage partners. Those who know themselves to be sinful human creatures loved by God may be moved to confess their shortcomings and to extend forgiving love to each other. Without being unrealistic, they believe in each other's highest possibilities and work optimistically for mutual growth. Marriage becomes a channel for the expression of God's steadfast love. The events of everyday family life in prosperity or adversity become a means of grace. "If we love one another, God lives in us, and his love is perfected in us" (1 John 4:12b).

What do you believe God intends for couples in terms of their growth and the enrichment of their marriages?

How have you seen God working in the lives of couples in crisis?

3

BASIC GOALS FOR MARRIAGE PREPARATION MINISTRIES

"Hold to the standard of sound teaching" (2 Timothy 1:13).

While helping couples consider their readiness for marriage and ways to nurture their continuing growth, there are at least six specific goals you will want to keep in mind:

- to help the couple understand the nature of marriage from the perspective of Christian faith;
- to enable each partner to better understand him- or herself and what he or she brings to the marriage;
- to surface expectations and prepare the couple for the adjustments they must make in marriage;
- to help them discover their strengths and their growing edges;
- to train couples in the use of effective communication skills;
- to establish or strengthen a pastoral relationship with the couple.

These goals are not separate items to be worked on one at a time or in a particular order. They are interrelated and overlap considerably; but each area is important and should be explored in depth, according to the needs of individual couples. In addition, there are particular concerns to be addressed when working with couples who have been married previously, who already have children, who are cohabiting, or who come from different religious or ethnic backgrounds.

Understanding the Nature of Marriage

Even though you have in mind specific concepts you consider essential to a Christian interpretation of marriage, you must begin with a couple wherever they are in their understanding. In most cases you will start by focusing on the wedding. Most couples come to you primarily to prepare for that event, perhaps with little thought or concern about the marriage relationship. If they are not part of your church family, you might inquire why they want to be married in a church and by a clergyperson—and why they have chosen you. In the course of your first meeting, you will want to ask in a gentle and non-threatening manner what they consider to be most important for marriage in general and for Christian marriage in particular. You can quickly assess whether the couple is comfortable with religious language or whether you need to use a more subtle approach. In Chapter 4, you will find specific questions you can ask to open up this area of discussion.

In addition to considering the couple's beliefs about marriage, you will want to share basic information concerning the normal stages of married life and the nature of love. David Augsburger, in *Sustaining Love: Healing and Growth in the Passages of Marriage*, describes four stages of marriage, each roughly equivalent to a decade in a couple's age span:

• the dream of the 20s,
• the disillusionment of the 30s,
• the discovery of the 40s,
• and the depth of the 50s.

The actual age of couples in those stages varies, of course, especially in this generation of later marriages. The time spans vary also. Still, it is safe to say that couples who survive the testing and probing of the second stage may break through to a deeper respect for each other and a new understanding of how to balance intimacy and autonomy. From this base, they can work toward a fourth stage of profound devotion.[1] Other writers label these stages differently and even describe a different number of stages; however most agree that marriage is a process, not an event, and that love changes and evolves over time.

Young love, or being "in love," is a love directed at our own fantasies and our own expectations, not a love truly directed at another person. Real love can begin only when one person comes to know and genuinely care for the other as he or she really is.[2] Being "in love" can grow into genuine loving, which is what a successful marriage accomplishes.[3] Couples who have been forewarned may remember, when going through these transitions, that such changes in their relationship are not only normal, but necessary. Better yet, in a context of ongoing marriage education, couples can access support when they need it to help them grow through each stage, cultivating a deeper, more meaningful, and possibly more passionate relationship.

Understanding Self and Others

Premarital counseling should help persons become aware of what they, as individuals, bring to marriage. Theme One in the Couple's Manual provides a number of exercises and activities to help couples consider the backgrounds, attitudes, and beliefs that have contributed to their becoming who they are. The "Marriage Lifestyle Questionnaire" in the back of the Couple's Manual addresses other areas of self-understanding. You will need to work within the limits of each person's readiness as well as the limits of your expertise and time available. Some persons who come to you will demonstrate a fairly healthy and mature sense of self-awareness

and self-esteem. Others may grow considerably through experiencing acceptance and affirmation in their relationship with you.

Some may need to be referred for more intensive counseling or therapy, in which case you will try to help them recognize this need and understand the value of such additional service. For example, you might observe that one of the partners does most of the talking, while the other defers and has little to say for him or herself. These behaviors might suggest to you that issues related to self-esteem and control may cause increasing difficulty in this relationship over the years. You will want to help this couple look at their behaviors and underlying attitudes, and you might encourage them to seek further counseling, either now or in the future. Dealing with such challenging situations is much easier if you have a consultant with whom you can confer.

One aspect of personhood that is very important in self-understanding and in marriage is an individual's feelings about his or her sexuality. Due to cultural and family conditioning, many persons come to marriage with negative feelings about sex of which they are not even aware. They may need help surfacing these feelings and affirming that sex is one of God's good gifts and that sexual feelings are normal and wholesome. Others may need help in affirming their maleness or femaleness, not just in terms of gender, but in regard to what it means to be a man or a woman in our culture.

Gender role expectations have changed significantly during recent decades, but boys and girls still grow up in different social environments that shape their attitudes and behaviors. While girls are more likely to learn caring and nurturing behaviors, boys are more apt to be trained to compete and to control. Women, then, may avoid conflict in order to preserve intimacy, and men may avoid intimacy as a threat to their independence.[4] When under stress, a woman often wants to talk to someone who will listen while she sorts out what is going on and what she needs to do. Men, on the other hand, tend to detach from their feelings when facing a problem and look for something they can do about it. While neither approach is necessarily better than the other, men and women need to understand these instinctive differences and learn to respond with understanding instead of defensiveness.[5]

Particular couples, of course, may find that they do not fall quite so neatly into these categories. All persons have both masculine and feminine psychological characteristics. To become the whole persons God intends us to be, we must accept and integrate all aspects of our selves. This process, which psychologist Carl Jung called individuation, "is both the gift of God and the fruit of great effort."[6]

In exploring feelings about sexuality, you might discover that a person has had some homosexual experiences and is concerned about their effect on his or her marriage. Some may carry an exaggerated feeling of guilt as the result of one or two such contacts, which were a part of childhood or early adolescent sexual experimentation and nothing more. A few, however, more deeply troubled by an established pattern of continuing homosexual feelings and/or experiences, may be questioning just who they are as sexual persons. Depending on your own attitudes and skills, you may be able to counsel some of these persons, but it is important that you be honest with yourself as to how helpful you can be. If you are uncomfortable or uncertain, which will be evident to the person anyway, it is important to admit it and make a referral.

Individuals frequently come to marriage heavily loaded with intangible baggage. If you can help couples clarify and verbalize with each other some of their basic beliefs, values, and attitudes, you will contribute not only to each one's increased self-understanding, but also to the possibility of depth and growth in the marriage. Here again, the "Marriage Lifestyle Questionnaire" and the Couple's Edition Theme One will be helpful. Preparing for marriage is not intended to be primarily a search for self-understanding, but if two persons can realize and assess what they bring to their marriage, they will be better equipped to build a lasting and satisfying relationship.

Dealing With Expectations

Some couples approach marriage with unrealistic expectations. Their dreams of marriage may be excessively romantic and illusory. Some may look upon marriage as a solution to all of life's problems. Stimulated by our highly individualistic and pleasure-seeking culture, it is no wonder that so many persons think first of their own happiness and what they can get out of marriage, rather than about the other person and the relationship. Some persons are unrealistic, not only in what they expect, but in how they expect it to happen—almost automatically, without any effort on their part. They do not realize the intentionality and effort a good marriage requires.

Marriage itself is a challenging adjustment. In contrast to the freedom of single persons to make their own decisions, married persons must consider almost every move in terms of how their partner feels about it, or how it might affect the couple's life together. Although each person is still an individual, responsible for his or her own life, each is also responsible for the relationship. Many people approaching marriage do not fully realize the increase in obligations and responsibilities they will experience, in addition to the pleasures and privileges of married life.

Unrealistic couples may resist premarital preparation, fearing that talking about their relationship will somehow diminish their happiness. Other couples may be so business-like in their approach to marriage, working hard to keep everything under control, that they may feel they do not need any assistance. In either case, they need to experience your pastoral concern. Romantic feelings are an important aspect of a relationship, but must not interfere with responsible handling of the realities of marriage. In fact, premarital counseling can enhance the thrill and excitement of getting married and encourage the continuation of genuine romance in marriage. The purpose is not to dull the spirit, but to build around it a framework that will conserve, release, and increase the joy of genuine love.

Theme Two of the Couple's Manual provides exercises to help the couple become more aware of what each partner wants and needs. As they share hopes and expectations, you can help them negotiate how to deal with these in their marriage. This does not mean that one must give up what is important to him or her. Nor does it mean demanding that either one always gets what he or she wants. A healthy relationship involves two persons, each with a sense of self-worth and integrity, a genuine respect for each other, and a commitment to each other's good. You can teach them how to find "win-win" solutions to the differences between them. (Couple's Manual, Section 4.3). You might want to practice this problem-solving process with your spouse or a colleague before using it with a couple.

In a sense, everything that happens to persons from birth prepares them for marriage, one way or another. Hurtful experiences within the family of origin may make it difficult to achieve the mutually satisfying adjustments required by marriage. Different parental models for husband and wife roles may cause conflict for a newly married couple or cause underlying stress that may not surface for years. Even couples who feel the roles their parents assumed were appropriate may change their minds over time. We know more than one wife who started out trying to emulate her mother's homemaking, cooking from scratch and doing most of the housework herself, but then found that role confining as she grew in her career and community involvement. Teaching a couple to share feelings and negotiate changes in roles and expectations gives them tools they can use to fine-tune their relationship through the years.

Making Adjustments: Religion, Money, Sex

Several areas of adjustment merit some concentrated focus: *religion*, *money*, and *sex*, in particular.

Religion

The *religious faith* of the couple involves their beliefs and practices, their goals and purposes, their doubts and growing edges of faith. If they differ in these areas, you want to help them find points of agreement on which they can build. They need to think about how they can nourish their spirituality in the years ahead. Also important is a consideration of the moral and spiritual values they share—or differ on—and how they plan to express these in their daily living. Although you may want to recommend some resources to help them grow in this area, it is important not to squelch honest dialogue by preaching to the couple at this point. You may advocate for a particular position, but you should not try to impose your beliefs.[7] You want to enable the couple to share their religious views and questions and consider for themselves how they wish to grow.

A study by the Center for Marriage and Family at Creighton University provides insights on effective ministries with inter-church couples, relationships in which each partner belongs to a different Christian denomination or church. These conclusions would also apply, perhaps with even more emphasis, to inter-faith marriages, as well as to those with differences in ethnic heritage. Among the most significant predictors of marital stability are participation in joint religious activities, having few religious differences, and family approval of spouse at the time of marriage. Religion can be a bonding force in marriage, or it can be divisive if differences are not managed effectively. Finding effective treatment of religious issues sadly lacking in preparation for inter-church marriages, this study challenges churches to give priority to such couples, who now make up a significant percentage of all who marry.[8]

"Marriage preparation is a natural rite-of-passage, a key learning moment, in a couple's life together. It can also be a key religious/spiritual moment. . . . Only 24 percent of interchurch couples reported having received special materials dealing with their different religious backgrounds. Providers of marriage preparation and enrichment programs should create programs attractive to and tailored to the needs of interchurch couples. These programs should highlight religious faith and practice as an important part of marriages and provide couples with tools to deal with their religious differences. Such marriage preparation may be done best when the denominations of the two partners are both represented."[9] Excellent resources for interfaith marriage preparation, including guidelines for planning the wedding ceremony and practical advice for confronting prejudice, dealing with in-laws, and raising children in a bicultural family, can be found through the Dovetail Institute and in the book *Mixed Matches: How to Create Successful Interracial, Interethnic, and Interfaith Relationships*, by Joel Crohn (See Resources).

Money

Money is mentioned by many couples as a major cause of conflict in marriage. In the case of younger couples, poor families, or those for whom employment is unstable, the lack of money is a problem itself; quarrels over finances, however, are frequently a symptom of deeper conflict, such as a power struggle. The ability to spend money as we choose is often a measure of our self-esteem, but marriage requires spending money on joint obligations. Disagreements over expenditures can escalate into outrage when partners feel their personal worth diminished by limitations on their ability to spend in accordance with their perceived needs.[10]

Exploration of attitudes and feelings about money may uncover some surprises. The Couple's Manual (Section 3.2) provides thought-provoking suggestions and exercises that can help get these feelings out in the open so that the couple can work on them together. You may also want to help the couple make intentional decisions about spending and evaluate their lifestyle in the light of their religious faith. Christian stewardship reminds us of our accountability to the rest of the world and to future generations, prompting us to make responsible decisions about our use of natural resources, our eating habits, and our spending. Again, while you may make some suggestions, it is most important that the couple share honestly with each other and learn to negotiate their differences.

You may, on occasion, be asked about prenuptial agreements regarding current or anticipated financial assets. Such agreements are typically drawn up when at least one of the parties has been previously married, when there is a significant age difference between husband and wife, and/or when there is a sizable difference in wealth or indebtedness. Perhaps the most common use of such agreements is when couples wish to protect the inheritances of their children from former marriages. Generally there would be no real reason for a young couple marrying for the first time to consider a prenuptial agreement, and certainly a couple's discussion of the disposal of their assets in case of divorce could become a self-fulfilling prophecy. Unless you have specific training in this area, couples who need to formulate such an agreement should see a lawyer.

Sex

Talking with a couple about their *sexual adjustment* usually has these goals: to provide a climate that will free them to talk about any sexual attitudes and practices they wish to discuss; to encourage a Christian attitude toward sex; and to make available specific information and resources in this area, according to the couple's needs.

The most important factor in providing a climate for the free discussion of sex is your own attitude and the extent to which couples experience you as a person with whom it is easy to talk. You want to project a genuine and helpful concern for persons—not a judgmental or condemning attitude. You will not be shocked, for example, by learning of premarital sexual activity, nor will you probe into areas that a person is not ready to explore. By sensitively picking up on and reflecting attitudes that may only be hinted at in words, you can help persons feel understood and appreciated, thus freeing them to move into examination of deeper feelings.

This does not mean that you give up on the ideal of premarital chastity. Certainly you will encourage those couples who have not yet engaged in intercourse to wait until after their wedding. In some cultures the engagement period has been a time for exploring all dimensions of a relationship: emotional, intellectual, and physical. Premarital sex and living together before marriage might be considered an extension of such practices. Traditionally, however, we have understood God's plan for us to include premarital chastity. There are also sound practical reasons for premarital abstinence. The fear of AIDS and other sexually transmitted diseases puts a different light on so-called sexual freedom. Premarital sex, moreover, can create a false sense of intimacy and distract a couple from important relationship-building tasks, such as learning to communicate feelings and resolve differences. Sexual fidelity is an art "dependent upon disciplines and practices learned and sustained over time," and couples might benefit more from the practice of keeping their promises than from the satisfaction of their sexual hunger.[11] Couples should be prepared for the probability that their sexual desire for each other will ebb and flow over time and that they may find themselves attracted to other persons. Coping with such experiences requires intentionality and deep commitment to the marriage partner and relationship.

Challenging couples to practice chastity throughout the marriage preparation period, whether or not they have already engaged in sexual intercourse, gives them the opportunity to focus on building true intimacy and on developing the skills they need to make their relationship work. In "A Case for Abstinence," Harriet McManus comments, "Building a relationship based on values, commitment and faith takes time, effort, and discipline. Premarital sex . . . inappropriately bonds a couple to self-gratification and becomes an inadequate substitute for meaningful dialogue that enhances growth."[12] One young man who participated in a premarital chastity covenant later reported that it was the best step he and his fiancée had ever taken: "I realize now that when we had an argument we would become physically involved to restore the sense of intimacy. By holding the physical element aside, we were forced to talk through the issues we needed to discuss. We found a deeper basis for the marriage—genuine compatibility, rather than a hollow sense of intimacy based on sex."[13]

Some pastors and counselors even advocate that cohabiting couples move apart and live separately until after the wedding. Although many cohabiting couples do eventually wed, there are significant differences between living together and being married, and cohabitation has not proven to be a reliable test of marital compatibility. According to a University of Wisconsin study, 40 percent of cohabiting couples break up before getting married, and for those who marry, divorce rates are 50 percent higher than for those who have never lived together.[14] Cohabitors "expect less mutuality and sharing of resources, friends, leisure activities and goals." Behaving more like roommates and giving less priority to their relationship, cohabitors often develop behavior patterns that do not translate well into marriage.[15] These issues should be clearly addressed in marriage preparation.

Even though many of the persons coming to you for marriage preparation are likely to have had sexual intercourse, most of them may still need some help with attitudes toward sex. In spite of the sexual freedom in today's society, past conditioning often hangs on in the form of negative beliefs. The overemphasis on sex in our contemporary culture often fosters an exploitative attitude of self-centered pleasure seeking, rather than the kind of pleasure-giving that nourishes companionship. Some persons come to marriage with unrealistic ideas about sex, which is so glamorized in our culture that couples may feel let down by the actual experience of intercourse. When their expectations of regular mutually-satisfying intercourse—including simultaneous orgasm—are not realized right away, they may be upset, feel inadequate, suspect that something is seriously wrong with them, or fear that they are incompatible. They need to be assured that it takes time, often weeks or months or even longer, for most couples to realize a good sexual relationship.

Couples who have been living together may blame the institution of marriage or even their choice of a mate for a decline in the intensity of their sexual interaction. In fact, such decline is a natural phenomenon and a necessary stage in the process of moving from infatuation to a more mature love. Deepening emotional connection over time can increase passion and sexual satisfaction. We believe it was David Mace who described the first two decades of marriage as a "twenty-year warm-up." That certainly comes over against our culture's expectation of instant gratification and the belief that sex is solely for the young!

If you feel uncomfortable discussing sexual matters, your embarrassment and uncertainty will be obvious. It is not wise to exceed your own limits. In whatever way you can, however, encourage a positive Christian attitude, one that affirms and appreciates sex as a good gift of God—not only for the purpose of procreation, but also for fellowship and communion between man and woman. "The husband should give to his wife her conjugal rights, and likewise the wife to her husband" (1 Corinthians 7:3). *Intended for Pleasure: Sex Technique and Sexual Fulfillment in Christian Marriage*, by Ed Wheat and Gaye Wheat, which is listed in the Resources section of this manual, might help to expand your thinking and increase your comfort in regard to this subject, as would several other books on the Marriage Education and Enrichment reading list.

You can recommend Section 3.3 in the Couple's Manual for exploration of this subject. You may also want to suggest one or more books to help the couple learn more about sexual technique, the emotional and spiritual aspects of sex, and how to deal with male and female differences in regard to sexual intercourse. Many pastors and counselors recommend that couples make appointments with a medical doctor for physical examinations, advice on birth control, and assistance in establishing a satisfactory sexual relationship.

Recognizing Strengths and Areas for Growth

Premarital counseling can help couples discover strengths on which they can build and areas of need that will require some attention and effort. By affirming and helping them explore their strong points, you increase their confidence and encourage them to continue nurturing positive aspects of their relationship. Within this context, you can assure them that every relationship has room for growth and share with them resources relevant to their particular needs. The questionnaire in the back of the Couple's Manual or some other premarital inventory will help to surface both strengths and those areas where growth is needed. See the Resources section for ideas.

Three strengths in particular that bode well for marital growth are a couple's desire to prepare for their marriage, their determination to make their marriage work, and an awareness of their need to grow. Some couples understand marriage to be an important and sometimes difficult undertaking. They may have learned from their friends and family, including their own parents, that a satisfying marriage does not just happen, but requires commitment to make it work. They may have been nurtured through the ministry of the church—through the ongoing curriculum of the church school, special seminars, personal experiences with married couples, and, of course, your sermons. They may be aware of current media coverage of conferences such as those held by Better Marriages, The Association of Marriage and Family Ministries and the National Association for Relationship and Marriage Education, various marriage education programs, and the work of researchers and therapists. These couples will appreciate all the help you can give them.

The second important strength, a determination to do their best to get the most out of their marriage, will greatly increase a couple's ability to benefit from premarital counseling and marriage education. These couples will not consider divorce an option, and in addition to learning from their work with you, they will also seek out resources for continuing growth through the years. The third important strength is an acceptance of human imperfection, which keeps us from expecting too much of ourselves and permits us to be more understanding of others. This does not mean passive resignation, but rather an acceptance of our shortcomings as a challenge to improve and grow.

When persons approaching marriage demonstrate sincere humility and an inner drive toward wholeness, as well as a desire for meaningful marriage preparation and a determination to succeed in their marriage, you will want to affirm and build on these strengths. For example, when a couple declares a commitment to fidelity, you might explore with them a broader understanding of that quality, helping them appreciate some dimensions they may not have thought of before. As a spiritual guide, you can point out that fidelity involves much more than faithfulness in sexual behavior. True faithfulness involves recognizing the sacred worth of one's partner and dedicating oneself to the partner's welfare, as well as one's own, working toward an egalitarian relationship.

Reassurance from you about their readiness for marriage, with specific affirmation of positive aspects of their personalities and relationship, will relieve some of the apprehension engaged couples are likely to feel, stimulating them to continue to grow in their relationship. At the same time, it is important not to gloss over problems and potential sources of difficulty. Some of these will surface through the premarital questionnaire or inventory, while others will be obvious right away. For example, although mixed marriages—interdenominational, interfaith, and interracial—have become much more common and are generally more readily accepted than by previous generations, such couples need to face realistically the tensions their differences may cause not only within their marriage, but also with others in the communities in which they live. You want to help them explore their motivation for marriage to be sure they are not driven by rebellion against their parents or by some other unsound reason. And you will want to strengthen their skills for dealing with whatever issues may arise.

In some situations you will want to spend time working on specific issues you see as potential difficulties for a couple. You might use certain activities in the Couple's Manual during your sessions, or recommend that the couple work on a specific section together and/or read relevant books or other material.

You may want to refer some couples to other professionals for assessment and assistance in regard to specific matters. A premarital consultation with a medical doctor, for example, could address general health concerns as well as specific matters related to sexual adjustment and contraception. Questions related to property and alimony carried over from a previous marriage may require legal advice. Some couples may need the services of a financial consultant to help them with long-range planning and with such issues as selecting health insurance, refinancing outstanding loans, or making wise investments. Financial and estate planning is especially important for older couples, who may need a lawyer's assistance for drawing up a prenuptial agreement to protect their children's inheritances from the standard practices of the state in which they reside. On occasion you may wish to refer persons to a psychotherapist, to a social service agency, to a mental health clinic, or to such self-help groups as Alcoholics Anonymous. You need to know what services are available in your community and nearby in order to make good use of them. Referrals should be handled in a sensitive manner so that persons come to see the real value of such consultation and can accept your recommendation as a positive step for their own benefit.

Improving Communication Skills

One of the major purposes of marriage preparation work is to facilitate and improve communication between the partners. Communication is the key to a deep and intimate relationship. Unfortunately most of us have only the limited skills learned in our families of origin, although more and more training is now being offered. By coaching the couple through some of the exercises in their workbook, you can help them practice effective ways to express themselves, to listen to each other, and to resolve conflicts. Their participation in experiential activities, as opposed to just reading or hearing about effective communication skills and techniques, increases the likelihood that they will actually apply these skills in their interactions when they are on their own.

In marriage preparation you can help a couple understand that communication is a two-way process. It is not a matter of one person merely "telling" the other something. A message does not get through unless the other is really listening and responding to what is being said. Much of the time one hears only one's own interpretation of a message, not what was actually meant. The listener must try to understand what the speaker means to say, and the speaker must try to convey clear information. When couples do not make an effort to hear what each other is trying to communicate and when they do not try to respond appropriately, the relationship suffers.

Because effective communication is best taught by modeling, you will want to practice making clear statements of your own ideas and feelings, as well as listening so that those with whom you interact feel truly understood (Couple's Manual, Sections 4.1 and 4.2). You may want to practice these skills with a colleague or with your spouse. Mentor couples (Chapter 8) should also be well trained in these areas. Group sessions can provide excellent opportunities for couples to practice effective communication skills (Chapter 9).

One mistake many couples make is interacting with each other only on the rational level, overlooking or neglecting the communication of feelings. For example, a wife's complaint about a problem may sometimes elicit advice from the husband, when all she really wants is empathy and the knowledge that he understands what she feels. In some families, in fact, children are taught to hide or suppress their emotions. Feelings that are not owned and accepted are likely to fester and worsen, causing distress to the individual and damaging relationships between persons, perhaps without either realizing what is causing the problem. When you help couples learn to be more sensitive to each other's feelings, they can experience the benefits of bringing both positive and negative feelings out into the open. Encourage giving affirmations (Couple's Manual, Section 4.4), sending accurate messages, and listening reflectively (Couple's Manual, Section 4.1) in the context of your premarital counseling and in group sessions. The good feelings generated by these activities will increase the likelihood of a couple's continuing use of these skills.

You can also help couples understand the role of nonverbal communication: gestures, facial expressions, posture, actions, and even silence. Because it is difficult to interpret and respond appropriately to the feelings behind such behaviors as slammed doors or withdrawal, couples need to talk things over. Couples who shut down areas of communication because they are uncomfortable dealing with feelings, or because their attempts at dialogue result in wounded feelings and make matters worse, lose the opportunity to build genuine intimacy. Because marriage is a dynamic, ever-changing relationship, couples need effective communication for dealing with the inevitable tensions and disagreements that arise in the normal course of living.

You will want to help couples discover some of the barriers that interfere with their communication. They may find themselves, in the rush of preparing for the wedding, failing to talk things over. One person may complain that the other does not really listen or take seriously what he or she is saying. The other may respond negatively to small talk and retreat from communication because of preoccupation with his or her own personal interests and concerns. Such feelings as guilt, insecurity, hostility, resentment—or even simple fatigue—can block communication. Couples may need to learn to postpone discussion of a problem until they can work on it more constructively, but such postponements should include a clear commitment to follow through, preferably at a specific time and place.

Within the context of counseling sessions, many opportunities will arise for you to encourage communication and coach the couple in using effective speaking, listening, and problem-solving skills. You can suggest that the woman tell the man how she feels about an issue using an "I-message," gently reminding her to rephrase any blaming or attacking statements. You can ask the man to give feedback about what he understands her to have said before he expresses his own opinion, and encourage him to guess at what she might be feeling. You might "assign" use of a problem-solving process in which they each express all their thoughts and feelings on a subject and carefully listen to understand each other before freely brainstorming possible solutions that will meet both of their needs (Couple's Manual, Section 4.3). Even better, take the time to actually coach them through this process so they can see how it feels. Emphasize that even with the best possible communication training, they will at times—especially under stress—revert to their old instinctive patterns. The skill training, however, will help them analyze what went wrong, correct themselves, and reapproach the problem more effectively.

Many people shy away from conflict if they can avoid it. You can put a couple at ease by assuring them that conflicts are normal in intimate relationships and that they can find ways to negotiate differences. More important than the resolution of any particular conflict that may emerge in the course of premarital counseling is helping the couple overcome their fears and learn to accept conflicts as opportunities for growth.[16]

Finally you may need to help couples evaluate their effectiveness in problem solving and recognize when they need to seek outside, perhaps professional, help. The following six guidelines clarify when couples should seek such assistance:

- When they are unable to agree that a problem exists; one is very upset, but the other does not appear to be concerned.
- When they both agree that there is a problem, but they are unable to define it.
- When they try to work through the steps of the problem-solving process but are unable to get anywhere.
- Whenever communication breaks down and they simply cannot discuss a problem.
- When their efforts to improve their relationship only make matters worse.

Be sure to point out to the couple the self-test in the Couple's Manual for determining the need for professional help (Explore 2.3G).

Strengthening the Pastoral Relationship

If you are perceived as understanding and helpful during marriage preparation, and if you establish a clear understanding of marriage as a growth experience with many surprises along the way, hopefully the couple will feel comfortable asking for further help as needed in their marital journey. Some pastors actually schedule follow-up appointments at a set interval, such as six months to a year after the wedding, or strongly encourage couples to participate in seminars or retreats for newlyweds. This practice reflects Dr. David Mace's observation that six months after the wedding is a prime time for working with couples on relationship issues.[17] Follow-up sessions or reunion gatherings of couples who have met together during the engagement period can be an effective way to stimulate ongoing growth, especially if mutual trust and openness has been cultivated in their gatherings. Mentor couples who meet regularly with newlyweds through the first year or two of marriage may actually be more effective than you can be, because of the personal relationship they establish over time.

To some extent a relationship may be carried over from one pastor to another. From a good experience in preparation for marriage, a couple may generalize that pastors care about persons and their relationships and that they are capable of giving help. (See "The Pastor-Couple Relationship" in Chapter 1.) Unhappily the opposite is also true. Clergy who do not take marriage preparation seriously give the impression that pastors do not care and/or that they are inept in ministering to marital needs. It is of even greater value for couples to experience the church, not just an individual pastor, as supportive and caring. Mentor couple relationships, other intergenerational friendships, and connections with other couples in their peer group can help to form an ongoing supportive community for newly married couples in your congregation.

PART TWO
WORKING WITH COUPLES

"By the power at work within us [God] is able to accomplish abundantly far more than all we can ask or imagine" (Ephesians 3:20).

4

THE PASTOR AND COUPLE— FIRST SESSION

"...being rooted and grounded in love" (Ephesians 3:17b).

At the first meeting with a couple, your goals should include:

- assuring the couple of your pastoral concern;
- establishing a counseling relationship;
- clarifying details about the wedding ceremony and the rehearsal;
- assessing what preparation the couple has already made for marriage;
- enlisting the couple's participation in marriage preparation activities.

Some couples will eagerly participate in premarital counseling sessions and marriage preparation programs, while others will be interested only in getting them over with. All can benefit in some way as long as certain basic elements are included. This chapter and those that follow present models you can use for developing your own marriage preparation ministry. Depending on the resources available, you will want to decide on a basic plan that can be adapted to different situations. Some activities described in this chapter, you will note, could be dealt with by a mentor couple or in a group setting. (See Appendix V, "Guide/Checklist for Marriage Preparation.")

Think through how you will respond to those who question mandatory participation in marriage preparation programs. Mike McManus recommends that churches require at least four months of premarital work with couples.[1] David Olson and others who worked with him in the development of the PRE-PARE inventories report that marriage preparation is most effective when it begins at least a full year before the wedding.[2] To parents complaining about a church policy that in effect forced their daughter and her fiance to postpone their wedding plans in order to meet marriage preparation requirements, Scott Stanley suggested responding, "Why would these parents want their children's marriages to be at greater risk?"[3]

Regardless of how intentional you are about providing for adequate marriage preparation, on occasion you will need to compress much into a few days and make critical decisions about what to insist on and what to omit. While some pastors may feel inclined not to marry those for whom adequate preparation time is impossible, others prefer to be flexible enough to extend grace and loving pastoral care to all.

Initial Contact

The first contact in regard to marriage preparation is often a phone call from an individual or family member inviting the pastor to officiate at a wedding and/or requesting to use church facilities on a date that has already been determined. Persons who make such requests well in advance, wanting to be sure that a desired date will be available, make it easier to arrange adequate marriage preparation.

After confirming your availability and that of the church sanctuary for the wedding date, you can immediately set up an appointment for your first session with the couple.

Sometimes a request for the use of the church and for your participation in a ceremony comes from a couple who like the appearance of the church building or who have heard good things about you, but with whom you are not familiar. Some pastors ask such callers to identify themselves after a regularly scheduled worship service, at which time the wedding date and first premarital session may be scheduled. This, of course, acts as a screening process limiting your marriage preparation ministry to those couples willing to at least consider being part of the Christian community, if that is your desire.

Persons who are part of your congregation may already have some idea of what to expect. A church can create a positive climate for marriage preparation by offering a comprehensive marriage ministry program, which might include celebrative occasions for married couples and families, marriage enrichment and marriage encounter events, ongoing support groups, mentor couple programs, relationship education for all ages, and sermons touching on marriage and family life. Publicity about upcoming opportunities for engaged couples and occasional notes in the bulletin or newsletter can remind people to make early arrangements for weddings in order to provide time for adequate marriage preparation. If your church is part of a community marriage agreement, you will experience the additional support of being part of a larger community that takes marriage and marriage preparation seriously.

A printed statement explaining the church's policy and practices in regard to weddings, expectations of those who use the church for weddings, and the various marriage preparation programs available should be given to the couple. The worship committee or administrative council may wish to develop a statement covering questions about decorations, music, picture-taking, and so forth, in order to avoid distractions from the worshipful nature of the service. (See Chapter 10, "Marriage Preparation Policy and Practices," for suggestions for developing such a document.)

Some congregations hold ceremonies for newly engaged couples to affirm the seriousness of marriage preparation and ritualize the commitment of the whole church to this ministry.[4] (See Appendix I for a sample liturgy you might use within congregational worship or in some other setting.)

Some pastors give the Couple's Manual or other reading material to engaged couples even before their first premarital counseling session. If you have a group seminar or series established, or if there is an Engaged Encounter or similar program taking place (Chapter 9), you could ask the couple at the time of initial contact to seriously consider participating. If you have a mentoring couples program in your church (Chapter 8), you might explain that concept and how they can be matched with a more experienced couple for mentoring activities; or you could wail until your first meeting with them for this discussion.

You will no doubt be informed early on if the couple wishes to involve other clergy with you in the wedding, perhaps a childhood friend, a relative, or a pastor from another denomination. You should contact any such person immediately to clarify the roles each of you will play both in the ceremony itself and in the couple's preparation for marriage.

Structuring the First Session

Try to schedule at least an hour and a half for this first session. It is critical to get started with both the man and woman present, if possible, so that they will feel they are preparing for their marriage together. This also protects each partner from any feeling that you have set up an alliance with the other one, an even more crucial matter if one is from another church or another town. Having them come together communicates that you identify them as a couple. Being together may make it easier for them to focus on their relationship and to support each other in this new situation. Couples are usually uncertain enough about counseling and anxious enough about getting married without having to cope with the feeling of aloneness.

Meeting with the couple together also gives you an opportunity to observe how they relate to each other. Perhaps the most important reason for seeing them together at first, however, is because of what happens to the couple as they share the experience. Each may stimulate the other to make particularly significant responses. They may raise questions with each other that they might not have discussed before, and that may prompt a deeper kind of sharing. This kind of exchange is also likely to stimulate deeper communication outside the counseling sessions. If, however, you can see them together only just before the wedding, you will need to find ways to encourage their participation in ongoing growth experiences afterward.

From the initial contact through your first counseling sessions, you will be involved in a process called "joining." This means developing a good working relationship with the couple, as individuals and as a unit, so that they will consider you a competent guide who can help them achieve their goals and whose suggestions and advice they will heed. You want to create positive expectations that the work you do together can really make a difference in their marriage relationship. Generate confidence in your professionalism by starting and ending appointments on time and by greeting the couple as they arrive, indicating clearly where they are to sit. Have chairs arranged so that they are seated closer to each other than either is to you. If you are not already well-acquainted, establish immediately whether they wish to be called by their first names or not, and clarify how you would like to be addressed. Lean toward them as they speak, and look at your watch only while you, not they, are talking.[5]

Some initial conversation will be needed to establish rapport with the couple, depending on the extent to which you already know either or both of them. Some simple, easily answered questions might include:

- *How long have you known each other?*
- *How did you meet?*
- *When did you first decide that he or she was the one for you?*
- *When did you get engaged?*

How you ask questions and how you listen and respond to the couple is critically important. By demonstrating your personal interest in them with care, respect, acceptance, and affirmation, you build a climate of trust in which open communication can take place. (See Chapter 1 for a fuller discussion of the "Pastor-Couple Relationship.") You might also ask them how they feel about being in this setting, assuring them that some discomfort in such situations is common. Helping them to be aware of and to express their feelings may relieve some of their anxiety.

You also need to let the couple know early on what to expect in this initial meeting and in the following sessions. Providing this structure through a process of negotiation is more effective than dogmatically insisting they follow a previously established plan. However, without some sense of organization, couples may feel at sea in an unstructured counseling session. Along with flexibility and freedom, they need to feel that what is happening is part of a plan and that there is some direction to it. They need to have assurance that you know what you are doing and where the sessions are heading.

Recordkeeping

Because so much may happen during a session, keep clear, well-written records. During the session you may simply jot down key words or topic sentences, but take time shortly afterward to fill in with more complete statements and to note what you want to pick up on next time. Without good records, it is easy to forget essential details or to confuse one person or couple with another. With some couples, these records might be of value not only during the marriage preparation period, but also in any counseling sessions you might have months or even years later. Such records, of course, must be kept confidential and stored in a secure location. You might even want to use code letters or numbers instead of names on these records. The "Guide/Checklist" (Appendix V) may be copied and used for planning and to keep track of what you do with each couple.

Wedding Details

The Wedding Information form in the GROWING LOVE IN CHRISTIAN MARRIAGE Couple's Manual serves as a tool for providing you with basic information about the couple's wedding plans. This is often the most comfortable place to start the first meeting with a couple, although you may want to ask them to fill it in beforehand and bring it to the first session so you can photocopy it. The couple may have many questions about the rehearsal or the reception, and the ceremony itself. If your church has prepared a wedding guidelines document as described above, you can share that at or before the first session. By starting with the couple's immediate concerns and responding to their questions directly and clearly, you demonstrate that you care about them and that you will be helpful.

During this first session or a later one, you will want to read through the wedding ritual with them. Unless the words are reviewed carefully in the premarital counseling session, they may not be heard at the wedding. Two weeks after marrying Sue and John, a pastor performed another ceremony at which John was an usher. During the reception, John asked the pastor, "Did you use a different service today from the one you used at our wedding?" When the pastor assured him that he had used exactly the same ritual, John looked at him with a puzzled expression and then grinned. "No kidding!" he exclaimed. "Did I really agree to all that?"

As you read through the service with the couple, explain that they need not worry about where to stand or when to join hands or exchange rings, as those instructions will be given during the rehearsal. This is a time for concentrating on the words, on what it means to be married according to these vows. Encourage them to interrupt at any point to ask questions or make comments. If they do not ask questions, you might point out several of the most important statements or explain some of the symbolism in the ritual, in light of the theological perspectives discussed in Chapter 2. If the couple is not part of your church family, you may want to consider the suggestions under "Faith Issues" in Chapter 4 before attempting an in-depth discussion with them.

If the couple wants to plan their own ceremony or add touches of their own, you can help them design a worship service celebrating the values discovered in their exploration of the meaning of marriage which follows. Such considerations are particularly important when there are differences in the couple's religious experience and heritage. You might offer them Andy Langford's *Christian Weddings: Resources to Make Your Ceremony Unique*, which provides options for the different elements of wedding liturgy or when appropriate, *Interfaith Wedding Ceremonies: Samples and Resources* (see Resources).

Faith Issues

You will have some sense early on as to the couple's level of comfort with religious language and faith-related issues. If you have a long-term relationship with them through church activities, faith issues and religious language will be a natural part of your conversations. If they are strangers to you, you may want to inquire as to their reasons for asking a pastor to perform their ceremony and learn what you can about their personal histories in terms of church affiliation and participation. You might also point out the difference between a civil service that would join them in a legal contract and a religious ceremony in which they commit themselves to a covenant relationship. If you have not already given them copies of the GROWING LOVE IN CHRISTIAN MARRIAGE Couple's Manual, you might want to do so now and suggest they read the material in "Perspectives on Marriage." If one of them is of another faith, however, you will need to ask that person what understandings he or she has of the meaning of marriage from a faith perspective. When working with a couple with different religious backgrounds and experiences, help them to talk about what they have in common and how they can build on that. In a later session with them, you might help them apply the problem-solving process from Section 4.3 in the Couple's Manual to deal with some of their differences. See "Resources for Marriage Preparation Ministries" for resources you can use with or recommend to interfaith couples.

You can work most effectively with a couple by beginning at their level of comfort. The extent to which you incorporate prayer and refer to Scripture will be determined by what you understand to be meaningful to them. Depending on the experiences a couple has had in Christian communities and their level of comfort with religious language, you may use some or all of the following questions to begin discussion about the meaning of marriage for them. (The italicized questions suggest what you might listen for in their responses.)

1. What is marriage?

Do they understand it as a lifelong union based on love and loyalty? Do both partners intend their marriage to last "till death us do part"?

2. What is love?

Do they understand that love, in this context, does not refer to a feeling, but to a decision to care for the other with a self-giving love—sacrificing, forgiving, sustaining, affirming love, freely given? Does their understanding of love include a positive attitude toward sex as a good gift from God?

3. What is fidelity?

Do they understand what it means to "forsake all others"? In addition to the more common understanding of sexual fidelity, you might want to refer this to the scriptural account in Genesis 2:24. What will it mean for them to shift their primary loyalty from their family of origin to the new union they are establishing? How can they balance honoring their parents with their responsibility to their new family unit?

4. What is the relationship between your faith and your marriage?

In choosing to marry each other, do they feel they are responding to God's will for them? How do they discover God's will for their lives? To what extent have they each made a personal commitment to God as revealed in Jesus Christ? If their level of commitment is different, how will they deal with that difference? If one of them is of a different faith, what does that faith have in common with Christianity? What differences are there? What importance do they place on being part of a faith community? What importance do they place on showing concern for others, moving beyond their own needs and satisfactions to involvement in service to the world?

5. What does it mean to talk about marriage as a covenantal relationship?

Are they committing themselves not only to a life-long union, but also to growing in love, to a continuing effort to achieve a quality relationship? Of what resources for nurturing their love are they already aware? Do they understand their relationship to be one between equals, recognizing each other as a unique individual created by God?

6. What is the overall goal of your life together?

What do they understand to be God's will for them? What do they believe is the highest value in this life? How do they plan to realize this value as a couple? What do they believe will give the deepest meaning to their marriage?

Assessing the Couple's Preparation for Marriage

During this first session, inquire about what preparation they have already made for marriage. Either or both may have taken courses or read books related to the subject. Ask them what they have found help-

ful—or not helpful. Have they had medical examinations recently, or have they considered doing so? Have they consulted with professionals regarding financial planning? Health insurance? Family planning? Legal matters, such as wills or child custody issues? Encourage them to identify and assess their need for further preparation, as individuals and as a couple. This is not a time to probe for problems, however. Problems will surface at the appropriate time, if a sound relationship is established and if the couple feels confident you will not pressure them to reveal more than they are ready to share.

Using Premarital Inventories

(This activity could be conducted by a mentor couple.)

One of the best ways to discover how to be of specific help to a couple is to use a premarital inventory, such as the Marriage Lifestyle Questionnaire, in the back of the GROWING LOVE IN CHRISTIAN MARRIAGE Couple's Manual. In the twenty or thirty minutes it takes to fill out the forms, the couple gives you information that would take hours to share in conversation. The questionnaires give each person an opportunity to become involved, in a serious, systematic way, in marriage preparation. Filling out the questionnaires often motivates people to work on areas they had not previously considered important. Questionnaires also enable you to sort out a few major areas on which you can concentrate attention in the remaining interviews. They give you an overview of pertinent influences in each person's background and some insights into the ways they are adjusting to each other. Even more important is the communication that will be stimulated between the partners when they compare their responses and share feelings with each other.

If mentor couples have not been trained to conduct this activity, it is probably best to ask the couple to fill in the forms while they are in your office, perhaps at the end of the first interview. This ensures that each person answers the questions without consulting the other and that the completed questionnaires are left with you. If necessary, however, they can be taken home to be completed. You can remove them from the couple's workbooks and give them self-addressed envelopes for returning them to you in plenty of time before your next session, in order to give you adequate time for reviewing them. You might assign a code for each, if you have coded your confidential files. Again, caution each to complete his or her form without consulting with the other. After completing them, however, they should be encouraged to discuss their responses as much as they like.

Introducing the Couple's Manual

(This activity could be conducted by a mentor couple and/or in a group setting.)

Spend some time looking through the GROWING LOVE IN CHRISTIAN MARRIAGE Couple's Manual with them; point out how it is organized and ask them which sections seem most interesting and meaningful for them. If you actually engage them in one or more of the Explore exercises in Section 1.1 or elsewhere, they may feel more comfortable doing other exercises on their own. Another approach would be to have prepared for them an envelope with each of the topics for Explore 1.2A written on a separate slip of paper. Encourage them to draw one at a time for sharing during a walk or a meal or another relaxed time together. Depending on their willingness, you might suggest certain sections of the Couple's Manual to be completed before your next session with them. Or you might propose use of a devotional book or some other reading that would address relevant issues for them (See Resources section reading lists). Be mindful, however, that the pressure of wedding preparations may make it difficult for them to find time for much else. Giving small assignments that they can reasonably complete is preferable to setting them up for failure. Remind them to bring their workbooks to your next session with them or to their mentor couple meetings.

Plans for Next Steps

Before ending the first session, you will want to establish clearly what happens next. Show them the Engagement Liturgy (Appendix I,) and discuss an appropriate time for holding such a ceremony, if that interests them. If you will be meeting separately with the man and the woman (Chapter 5), schedule those appointments and clarify any expectations. You will usually want to meet with the couple at least one more time before the wedding (Chapter 6), and

you may plan to meet with them after the wedding (Chapter 7) as well. State your expectations clearly early on and proceed with booking those appointments, if possible. If you have a mentoring couples program (Chapter 8), hopefully you will have won this couple's interest and willingness to participate. If you have group sessions scheduled for engaged couples within your congregation or parish, or if you know of an Engaged Encounter Weekend coming up, hopefully they will agree to take part (Chapter 9). If you already sense that the couple will need additional sessions for a particular reason, you might say so or you may prefer to leave that discussion until your next session.

You may also invite the couple to consider a premarital chastity covenant. You do not need to know their present level of sexual involvement, although they may have already shared that information with you. Simply challenge them to decide to abstain from intercourse until after the wedding and help them to understand how this can deepen their relationship. You can find more information about and suggestions for such covenants in *A Manual to Create a Marriage Savers Congregation*. They can discuss this further with a mentor couple; you do not even have to know what they decide.

Closing

By the end of this session, you should have some idea about the couple's attitude toward matters of faith and some sense of what would be an appropriate way to end your time together. If the couple appears to be comfortable with religious language and practices, you can confidently invite them to join hands and pray with you as you bring the session to a close. You might praise God for the gift of love received by these two and for the uniqueness of each individual. You might thank God for the honor of being invited to share in their journey, asking for grace and wisdom to work well together and for guidance in regard to any particular concerns that may have surfaced. If they have been active in prayer groups or other spiritual activities, you could ask them to add their own words of prayer or to suggest what they would like you to include in the prayer.

If you suspect they might be uncomfortable with overtly religious practice, embrace them warmly or shake hands and assure them that you will pray

THE PASTOR AND COUPLE—FIRST SESSION

for them throughout this time of marriage preparation and through the beginning of their married life. Obviously you will not try to use prayer to convince them of something or to try to win them over to your point of view, even subtly. Hopefully, regardless of their previous experiences, the couple will have felt God's love communicated through your care. In any case, walk to the door with them and repeat the date and time for your next appointment.

Follow-up and Preparation

Set aside time to review and add to your notes as soon as possible. Amplify the key words and topics you have recorded to provide clear statements that will make sense to you after time passes and other encounters take place. In particular, note issues you want to be sure to address again or matters you may not have dealt with during this first session. Review the goals and suggestions in Chapter 3 of this manual. Copy the checklist in Appendix V of this manual to use for planning and for keeping track of your work with each couple.

If you have used the GROWING LOVE IN CHRISTIAN MARRIAGE questionnaires, privately compare the couple's responses, once you have them, checking for agreements and differences, item by item. With some experience and careful concentration, you should be able to do this in less than half an hour. Agreements may indicate strengths to be affirmed and developed. Differences may suggest problems that will require further attention. See Chapters 5 and 6 for specific suggestions for reviewing their responses with the couple. Most such discussions should take place with the couple together, but you may want to address some matters with either or both individually (Chapter 5). You can note items to be discussed in the margins of the questionnaires as you compare them or use different colored highlighting pens to indicate agreements and differences. Look beyond simple facts to the possible significance of information given. For example, if the response to Question 13 indicates a family broken by death or divorce, you will want to ask the person to tell you more about that experience, how it affected him or her, and what influence she or he thinks it might have on the upcoming marriage.

Because of their interrelatedness, some questions should be viewed in clusters, such as the marital status of the parents (Questions 12-13) and those related to the individual's childhood (Questions 11, 14-16, 18-21). Another example of clustering would be questions related to disagreement (Questions 30, 32-33). Question 23, on the individuals' careers, should be considered in connection with Question 29, regarding children.

When comparing one person's responses to the other's, look for similarities and differences in role expectations (Question 31), interests and activities (Question 34), and perceptions in regard to agreements and disagreements (Questions 30, 32-33). A difference in responses to Question 30 may indicate a lack of communication or it may point to a difference in interpretation of the item. Very few couples actually agree on all these topics. A couple whose responses indicate much disagreement may have learned how to handle differences and be in a stronger position than those not aware of their disagreements. Many couples come to marriage with only superficial consideration of these topics, however and may need help to explore some of them at greater depth. Note relevant sections of the GROWING LOVE IN CHRISTIAN MARRIAGE Couple's Manual that you want to call to their attention.

If a mentor couple administers and reviews the questionnaire, clarify with them which responses and issues you will address and which they will handle. If you have used Prepare/Enrich or FOCCUS inventories (listed in "Premarital Inventories" in the Resources section), submit them for scoring according to procedures. Remember that the evaluation of their responses is only part of the process. Couples grow most by talking with each other about the issues surfaced by the use of an inventory. Prior to each future meeting with the couple, whether seeing them individually or together, schedule a half hour of preparation time to review your notes, the inventory responses, and appropriate sections of the GROWING LOVE IN CHRISTIAN MARRIAGE Pastor's Manual and Couple's Manual.

5

SESSIONS WITH INDIVIDUALS

"For it is God who is at work in you, enabling you both to will and to work for his good pleasure" (Philippians 2:13).

Goals for sessions with individuals include:

- strengthening the pastor's relationship with each individual;
- assessing the individual's preparation for marriage;
- focusing on concerns individuals might not easily discuss in couple sessions.

Although you may not always feel individual sessions are necessary, meeting with each person alone can be an important component of premarital counseling. Such sessions afford the opportunity for strengthening the counseling relationship with each of the partners as individuals. Here, even more than in couple sessions, the individual may come to feel that *the pastor cares about me as a person—about my feelings, my needs, my hopes—as well as our marriage.* Here you can concentrate your full attention on the individual, establishing a deeper, more personal relationship. Here the person may experience greater freedom to focus on his or her own feelings and on helping you understand what he or she means, rather than wondering how the partner is interpreting everything, as may be the case in couple sessions.

Individual sessions presented as part of the usual pattern for premarital counseling will be more readily accepted than specific requests to meet with one or both persons alone. If, after you have begun counseling with a couple, you ask to meet with them pri-

vately, they may feel that there is something wrong with either or both of them or with their relationship. Generally speaking, you should try to see the partner you do not know as well first in order to strengthen that relationship. If you know both parties equally well, scheduling these appointments can be a matter of convenience.

The focus of these sessions is on the individual's preparation for marriage. You can help each person review his or her readiness for marriage, identify needs for personal growth, and consider possible resources for addressing those needs. In these one-on-one sessions it may be easier for a person to bring up problems or issues that might be difficult to mention in the presence of the partner. Discussing such matters with you alone could help prepare him or her to talk about them with the partner later.

Procedure

Since the private appointment adds a new dimension to the counseling relationship, you want to do all you can to put the individual at ease. In a warm and friendly manner, let the person know that you are glad to see him or her and that you appreciate the privilege of sharing in marriage preparation. You can help a person feel more comfortable by being sensitive to his or her feelings, even negative feelings such as resistance to counseling or to the pastor. Resistance may arise because of a person's expectation that the pastor will not be accepting and understanding. If you can help the person acknowledge and express negative feelings, they will usually subside.

You can also put the individual at ease by stating the purposes of this session and pointing out some of the matters that may be discussed. These might include the premarital questionnaire or inventory, reading material you recommended earlier, or specific subjects suggested by the person or by you. Inviting the person to decide where to begin gives him or her a sense of control and allows discussion of what he or she wants to talk about. If nothing comes as a result of this invitation, you might proceed with the person's responses to the questionnaire or inventory or bring up a topic based on your review of the first couple session.

Marriage Lifestyle Questionnaire Responses

Before the session, you will have reviewed the couple's responses, noting items that seem to call for more discussion (Chapter 4). Generally it is most effective to point out differences between the two persons' responses when you have both of them together. However, a private session may be the best setting for discussing matters he or she might hesitate to address honestly in the presence of the other, such as confidence that the marriage will be happy (Question 35) or a specific request for help (Question 36). If an individual's response to Question 28 indicates disapproval of the marriage by either or both sets of parents, this would also be an important subject to explore, since parental disapproval negatively impacts the stability and health of a marriage.

If responses to Question 4 indicate a previous marriage that ended in divorce or death, you will want to assess the extent to which the person has processed that experience and healed from its wounds. If there has been a divorce, or even a broken engagement as indicated in Question 10, listen carefully to discern whether or not the person understands the role he or she played in this relationship breakdown. Those who place blame entirely on the other person are at risk for repeating their mistakes.

Other Topics

Other topics you might suggest for discussion during an individual interview might be related to childhood experiences and religious traditions (Questions 11-21). If the couple grew up in different churches, different faith groups, or even different ethnic or cultural settings, you might give each the opportunity to explore those experiences with you. Your purpose would be to help surface feelings, expectations, and hopes so that the couple will feel more comfortable discussing these matters with each other.

During an individual interview, you might want to explore each individual's attitudes and knowledge about sex before bringing this subject up with the couple. Living in a culture that glorifies sex, many young people assume they know all they need to know about sexual relations. Others come to the marriage with very little preparation in this area and without much help from their parents, especially if their parents have been too self-conscious and uncomfortable to discuss sexual matters openly. Even couples who have been living together or those who have been previously married may need some counseling in the area of sexual adjustment. If you do not feel comfortable discussing sexual matters, you can suggest a good book on the subject (there are several on the reading list in "Resources for Marriage Enrichment Ministries"), or you might make a referral to a competent medical doctor or to a clinic on family planning. See Chapter 3 for fuller discussion of goals for premarital counseling in this area.

If you suggested any reading or use of the GROWING LOVE IN CHRISTIAN MARRIAGE Couple's Manual during your first session with the couple, you might inquire about how that is going. Your interest will emphasize the value of such reading and of the workbook exercises and will encourage persons to find time to do more. The opportunity to tell you about their experiences will help them assimilate and utilize information.

Surfacing Potential Disagreement

If the above suggestions do not result in meaningful conversation you might try an imaginative challenge. One rather mature couple in their late twenties showed no sign of disagreement on their premarital questionnaires. In his meeting with the man, the pastor said, "You indicate that you have had no disagreements and that you do not expect to have any serious ones after your marriage. But let me ask you this: If you could imagine yourselves having even a minor disagreement over something, what do you think it might be about?"

After a few moments of quiet reflection, the man replied thoughtfully, "She might be too bossy." The pastor invited him to say some more about that, and slowly the man opened up and shared some facts and perceptions about his fiancee's family. Her father had died four years earlier, but his insurance and her part-time work made it possible for her to finish college. Her mother had been an invalid for several years. The man was proud of the fact that she had actually supported her family since her graduation three years earlier, and the couple planned to continue contributing to the support of her mother and younger brother after their marriage.

It was more difficult for him to explain that his fiancee had been like a father and a mother to the younger brother. "I guess I am a bit afraid that she might treat me the way she treats him," he sighed, as if relieved to have said this. "Sometimes I'm afraid she will be bossy with me." After further exploration of his feelings, the man reported, as if he had just realized it, that one of the qualities that had attracted him to her was her ability to manage things well. Then he added, with a shy smile, "But I don't want to be treated the way she treats her little brother."

During a post-wedding session with the couple, this man reported almost exuberantly that this conversation with the pastor had given him enough courage to talk with his fiancee about both his appreciation of her managerial abilities and his fear of her potential bossiness. He felt that being able to talk about this kept it from becoming a problem for them. If they had not discussed it, he would have been supersensitive to any hint of control from her and would have found ways to resist or strike back. The pastor reports that this concern probably never would have come up in a counseling session with both persons present. It took the safety and the comfort of a private session to free the young man to address this potential problem.

Sometime before the end of the private appointment, you need to decide whether to recommend one or more additional individual sessions—either with you or with some other professional person or agency. Of course when you make this recommendation, it may be rejected. You, however, are responsible for taking this initiative and at least sharing a perception that further sessions could be helpful.

Closing

In closing this session follow the same principles discussed in Chapter 4. Afterward, again, you will want to spend some time reviewing your notes and checklist, considering how you will proceed with the next session or sessions.

6

THE PASTOR AND COUPLE— ADDITIONAL SESSIONS

"... that your love may overflow more and more with knowledge and full insight"
(Philippians 1:9).

You will usually meet with the couple at least one more time before the wedding, even if you have a mentor couples program (Chapter 8) or group activities (Chapter 9) to supplement your premarital counseling. In some cases you might schedule several more sessions, if time is available and needed to accomplish three basic goals:

- consider progress on the tasks of marriage preparation;
- complete plans for the wedding;
- cultivate the couple's openness to participating in post-wedding marital growth opportunities.

In order to accomplish the purposes of this session or sessions, you might do some or all of the following, except, of course, those activities that are being dealt with by a mentor couple:

- review responses to the premarital inventory;
- discuss concerns that came up in the individual sessions;
- work on specific issues, such as budgeting, family planning, and religious life;
- use relevant sections in the GROWING LOVE IN CHRISTIAN MARRIAGE Couple's Manual;
- summarize what they have learned so far, establish priorities, and plan for continued growth.

By reviewing your notes and the marriage preparation checklist on each couple, you can recall areas of concern that surfaced earlier and/or remind yourself of what you have already covered and what you have left to be dealt with later. Coordinate with the mentor couple, if one is involved, to be sure you do not duplicate efforts.

Tasks of Marriage Preparation

The tasks of marriage preparation are usually not fully completed before the wedding, but couples need to make enough progress to provide a secure foundation for continuing growth. Even couples who demonstrate genuine love, personal self-awareness, and willingness to grow still have work to do. Tasks focused on their relationship with each other include deepening their commitment, developing common interests, and learning to communicate effectively and resolve conflicts. Tasks focused outward include cultivating appropriate relationships with other persons, extended family, and community groups of which they are a part.[1] If two persons have made some progress toward establishing a couple identity and are aware of the continuing work they need to do in each of these areas, you can affirm their strengths and confirm their readiness for marriage.

If you have hesitations about marrying them, now is the time to resolve how you will deal with that. Some couples, once they recognize the difficulties in their relationship, decide to cancel or postpone their wedding. If they still choose to marry, the hardest position for you to take would be an outright refusal to participate, but this may in some cases be your only recourse. In other situations you might compromise, agreeing to marry them if they will consider your recommendations for further counseling or professional consultation.

Finalizing Wedding Plans

It should not take long to review plans for the wedding itself, to be sure all arrangements have been made, and to determine any additional details needing attention. Be sure the couple brings you the license before the wedding, at least no later than the rehearsal. This could save an embarrassing delay of the wedding, since most states require you to have the license in hand before you perform the ceremony. You might check the "Wedding Information form" to be sure the information on it is complete and correct. While reviewing the wedding plans, listen carefully for hints of tension or unresolved disagreements between the couple or involving other members of the family. In such instances, affirm calmly that negotiating differences is part of marriage and coach the couple through some problem-solving discussion.

Because of the excitement and strain the couple will experience as the wedding day draws near, do all you can to reassure them that they do not need to worry about the details of the service. Explain that you will guide them through each step of the ceremony. If the couple plans to memorize their vows, assure them that you will be prepared to gently prompt, if necessary, and that this will not detract from the atmosphere of worship. Be sure, if they have written their own vows, that you have gone over these with them and that you have a copy in case they do need prompting.

This might also be a good time to remind the couple of the deeper significance of wedding traditions that will be part of the reception festivities. For example, when the bride and groom feed each other wedding cake, they symbolize their commitment to nourish each other, in the broadest sense. That meaning is often lost when couples stuff pieces of cake rudely into each other's mouths. Sometimes wedding reception festivities are coordinated by a caterer or disk jockey, in which case the couple should be encouraged to discuss with that person ahead of time which traditions they want included and which omitted from their reception.

Marriage Lifestyle Questionnaire Responses

(The mentor couple can conduct this activity.)

While reviewing the couple's responses on the "Marriage Lifestyle Questionnaire," point out areas of strength, such as common experiences in their families of origin (Questions 11-21), approval of the marriage by parents and other significant persons (Question 28), common expectations in regard to responsibilities (Question 31), common values (Question 30), and interests (Question 34).

You will also call attention to areas that may require some special attention and effort, areas they will need to work on as their marriage evolves. Usually it is enough to point out differences in their responses and ask them how they think this might affect their relationship. Alerting couples to the fact that tensions may be expected in certain areas prepares them so that they are not taken completely by surprise. If they understand why such tensions arise, they may be better able to proceed cooperatively and constructively in dealing with them. In addition, you can share with the couple valuable resources—books, programs, and organizations—for dealing with their areas of concern.

Marked differences in background and experience require special attention (Questions 11-21). Age may be a concern if the couple is very young, if they are old enough to be set in their ways, or if there is a wide difference in age between them. Depending on where the couple lives, difference in race or nationality could be an issue, not only because of differing expectations they may bring to the marriage, but also because of pressures from the community (see the reading list in "Resources for Marriage Preparation Ministries"). A great deal of give-and-take might be required if there is much difference in their religious, educational, or economic backgrounds. This might also be true if one person is an only child and the other comes from a large family.

Parental disapproval (Question 28), if not already discussed, needs to be faced by the couple together. Even when there is no disapproval, young couples may still need help realizing that they are establishing a new family and that their primary loyalty now is to each other and not to their parents. At the same time, couples need to learn how to help each other relate in healthy ways to their own and each other's relatives.

For couples marrying in their middle or later years, adjustments to other family members could center around their adult children, who might not approve of the marriage. In such cases, the children may be afraid the new mate will reduce their share of any inheritance that may be left; or they may feel that a parent's new relationship dishonors the memory of the other parent, whether deceased or divorced. Blended families with children, regardless of their age, will have specific issues and adjustments to make. (Resources for blended families are listed in the Resources section.)

Division of household responsibilities is a problem area for many couples. Check both persons' responses for agreement or disagreement on role expectations and attitudes about household tasks (Question 31). Look at their responses to Question 18 also, to compare the experiences they had while growing up. Even if you have raised this matter in individual sessions, it is important for them to discuss this together. You can help them consider equitable ways to share household responsibilities, especially when both are employed full-time. Remind them that their feelings about these responsibilities may change as time passes and their circumstances change. The most important thing is for them to be able to talk honestly and openly about their feelings and needs in this and in every other aspect of their life together.

Question 30 contains a number of possibilities for further work on disagreements. Compare those items checked in the first five columns with those checked in the last three columns. Unless there has been much discussion of an issue, responses in the earlier columns may be based on superficial information and will be subject to change over time. You will want to draw them out to share with you their perception of the significance of some of their disagreements and to report on what progress they may have made in dealing with them. Again, it is important to communicate that disagreements are normal in an intimate relationship and that what matters most is how they learn to cope with and resolve them. Questions 32 and 33 shed important light on the couple's conflict-management patterns and may indicate a need for specific focus on the attitudes and skills they bring to this area.

Based on your review of their responses to the pre-marital questionnaire, you may want to recommend that they work with certain sections of the GROWING LOVE IN CHRISTIAN MARRIAGE Couple's Manual. Share that information with the mentor couple, if there is one, as well. Again, the couple will be more likely to follow through with such suggestions if the pastor or mentor couple actually participates with them in the activity, modeling use of the exercises and coaching them through the process.

Addressing Specific Issues

The individual interviews may have surfaced concerns that should be addressed with both persons together. You might have encouraged one individual to initiate a particular discussion with the other, or to bring up the subject during this meeting. If that does not occur, you could ask if he or she has found an opportunity to discuss the matter, or you could bring up the subject yourself and encourage the couple to talk about it. Suggest that they face and talk directly to each other, rather than to you. Act as a coach, gently reminding them to use "I" messages and to give feedback about what they hear each other saying (Couple's Manual, Section 4.1).

If you asked them to review the GROWING LOVE IN CHRISTIAN MARRIAGE Couple's Manual on their own, ask them what they have found useful or interesting. Choose one or more of the exercises to do with them, such as Explore 1.4B or 2.1C. If a mentor couple is meeting with them and using the workbook, inquire about how that experience is going for them.

Tasks of Marriage

(The mentor couple could conduct this activity.)
Another approach is to review the couple's growth in regard to developmental tasks they face in marriage and in becoming a family. The couple themselves must accomplish these tasks, but you can help them to understand the challenges they face, and you can give them some guidance for working on them. The tasks—which are interrelated and not isolated from each other—arise from three roots: personal maturation (physical, emotional, and social) of each person; cultural expectations regarding married couples; and the values and goals of the couple.

The following list of tasks, adapted from the work of Evelyn Duvall[2] is listed here for your information but discussed more thoroughly in Chapter 7.

1. Developing and sustaining a faith-based lifestyle
2. Developing and maintaining effective communication
3. Providing the necessities of life
4. Managing finances
5. Establishing roles and responsibilities
6. Meeting personal needs
7. Planning for children
8. Adjusting to relatives
9. Making and keeping friends
10. Taking part in community life

Summarizing Learnings

From time to time invite the couple to reflect on what they have learned so far and in what areas they need to continue working. Ask them to list the strengths they have discovered, and affirm any that they overlook. Point out progress they have made, such as resolving specific areas of tension or disagreement. Remind them of resources they can access, such as specific exercises in the Growing Love in Christian Marriage Couple's Manual, other reading materials, or groups and activities in which they can participate. Emphasize the importance of communication and rehearse important guidelines, such as the problem-solving process and the power of forgiveness in Section 4.3 of the Couple's Manual. To be sure, admonitions usually do not bring about much change, but some couples may benefit from reminders that a good marriage requires effort, that they need to avoid taking each other for granted, and that their marriage is worth working on together.

Review whatever opportunities are available to them for nurturing ongoing marital growth after the wedding. Although you do not want to make them dependent on you, you do want to establish a basis for continuing ministry to and with them as needed. Some pastors regularly schedule appointments with couples six months after their wedding. Some leave the schedule more open, inviting the couple to call during the first six months, so that they can schedule the appointment when they feel it will do them the most good. This allows time for the couple to work on some adjustments on their own, to settle down with each other, knowing that help is available if they need it. Knowing that the pastor expects them to call during this time frame, one or the other may suggest, when a problem arises, that this might be an appropriate time to make the post-wedding appointment. Mentor couples can meet this need for ongoing nurture and problem-solving after the wedding through their continuing relationship with a couple and/or by organizing sessions for groups.

Some pastors and mentor couple teams convene groups of couples married within the same time frame for a retreat, a series of seminars, or ongoing support groups. You might also encourage the couple to participate in a church school class or fellowship group for married couples, either intergenerational or specifically for newlyweds. If the couple does not belong to your church or if they are moving to another community, encourage them to find marriage-nurturing activities wherever they are to live. Do what you can to help them establish a relationship to a new church or with groups or persons you may know in their new community. If they are going away to college, find out how to keep in touch with them and how to help them become involved in faith groups or marital growth activities on campus.

Closing

The more often you meet with a couple, either privately or as part of a group activity, the more deeply connected you will feel and the more knowledgeable you will be about their faith journey and how to appropriately end a session. Follow the suggestions for closing prayer in Chapter 4, depending on the couple's level of comfort with religious language. If this is your last session before the wedding, you might call attention to that fact and close with the "Blessing of the Marriage" prayer provided in the wedding service.[3] By structuring into your couple sessions and group activities opportunities for couples to pray together, holding hands and talking to God aloud or silently in their hearts, you increase the likelihood that they will continue such practices on their own in their life together.

7

NURTURING MARITAL GROWTH
AFTER THE WEDDING

"What we will be has not yet been revealed" (1 John 3:2a).

In some situations most of the "premarital" counseling may take place after the wedding. If premarital sessions have been impossible to schedule, for one reason or another, couple sessions, individual sessions, meetings with mentor couples, and groups for newlywed couples all can take place during the first year or two of marriage. In any of these settings, you can process the couple's responses to the premarital questionnaire, work through the GROWING LOVE IN CHRISTIAN MARRIAGE Couple's Manual, and/or work on the developmental tasks. Postwedding sessions differ from premarital sessions in that they deal with the "here and now" of the couple's marriage relationship. Some pastors feel this kind of counseling is actually more effective than prewedding sessions because it allows them to work with the couple's relationship in the context of the realities of marriage. Consequently you will want to offer postmarital growth opportunities for all newlywed couples for at least two years after the wedding, especially for those who missed some of the premarital experiences. Be sure to include in your postwedding ministries couples married elsewhere, but now settling down in your community.

Let the couple know of your continuing interest in them and their marriage, even if you have provided them with extensive prewedding counseling. The first few months of marriage are crucial, because this is when two persons are trying to adjust to each other and establishing patterns of relating that are likely to continue the rest of their lives. Even couples who have been living together will be adjusting to a new way of life, because the experience of cohabitation has proved to be quite unlike that of marriage. Generally more differences surface during the first six months than at any other period of marriage, and a newlywed couple may not have had much experience in making adjustments and in handling disagreements. Not only is this the time when they are most likely to need help; it is also a time when they are more amenable to learning. They are not yet set in their ways or resigned to living with their problems without doing something about them. If appropriate help is available, newlywed couples are more likely to discover creative and satisfying ways to relate to each other.

Keeping in Touch

If you have previously discussed a post-wedding session with the couple, take the initiative by reminding them that you are looking forward to meeting with them again. Although you do not want to pressure them, your assurance that most couples benefit from continued marital growth support is important for them to hear. If the couple initiates a postwedding session out of their struggle with a specific problem, you will, of course, be doing marriage counseling and will need to use problem-solving approaches as discussed in Chapter 1.

The Marriage Preparation Evaluation Form at the back of this manual provides another opportunity for checking in with a couple after the wedding. Make two copies of the form, modified as necessary for your particular situation, and give them to the couple several weeks or months after the wedding. Include a stamped, self-addressed envelope. You might also include a personal note expressing your regard for them, reminding them to schedule a follow-up session with you, and/or inviting them to participate in upcoming group events for couples.

Some pastors remember all couples they have married with cards and personal notes on their wedding anniversaries. The Foundations Newsletter for Newly Married Couples, published bimonthly, addresses different marriage relationship topic in each issue. (See Resources for website information, where pastors or mentor couples can place orders for five or more subscriptions at a discount; or you could design your own.) A newsletter would serve to briefly remind couples of skills they learned during premarital sessions with you, with mentor couples, or in group sessions. Such communications may be just the reminder a couple needs about how to relate to each other more effectively and can also include invitations to participate in ongoing marital growth activities. Another way to keep in touch is by recommending and loaning books that other couples have found helpful.

Developmental Tasks of Marriage

The tasks of marriage provide a framework for planning ongoing marital growth opportunities for couples, whether you meet with them in individual sessions, offer ongoing groups or seminars, or assign them to mentor couples for support and encouragement.

Developing and Sustaining a Faith-based Lifestyle

Couples need to work out a common philosophy of life, a moral and spiritual value system that motivates their life choices. They need to agree on religious practices in their home and on participation in the life and ministry of a church. The intermeshing of two different lifestyles can be very challenging,

especially if the husband and wife come from different religious backgrounds or differing levels of church involvement. Establishing a common religious philosophy and practice is perhaps the most difficult and the most important task a couple faces. It may take a long time and may never be fully achieved since life keeps changing, and faith is always in the process of growth. But you can help the couple understand this task to be the foundation of their life together, shaping their approach to all of the other developmental tasks.

Inquire about the devotional life of each person and their plans for spiritual growth after marriage. Encourage them to share daily devotions, perhaps giving them a book or other resource for this purpose. Review their individual histories of church activity and help them plan for their future church life together (Couple's Manual, Section 2.2). Praying with them during your sessions increases the likelihood that they will include prayer in their life together. On the other hand, if there are differences between them that make praying together uncomfortable, encourage them both to nurture their own spiritual growth, practicing whatever spiritual disciplines they choose, while at the same time respecting the other's needs and desires.

A couple with common experiences and inclinations in regard to religious belief and practices may easily embrace the idea that their marriage relationship can serve as a channel for God's love and a means of service to the world. They may already understand that God has a purpose for their marriage—including their ministries to each other, to their children, and to the communities of which they are a part. For couples less comfortable with religious language, you can ask: *What do you hope to have accomplished in ten, twenty, or thirty years or more? To what are you giving your lives?* This may be an entirely new way of thinking for them, and they may not know how to respond. Discussing their values, beliefs, and goals in life may help them begin to think about their marriage as a spiritual journey. (Couple's Manual, Sections 1.1, 1.4, 2.1, 2.2, 2.4, 3.1, 3.2, 3.4, and 3.5)

Developing and Maintaining Effective Communication

Couples need to communicate meaningfully with each other, both emotionally and intellectually. This requires give-and-take, not just one partner telling something to the other. Each partner needs not only to get the other's message, but also to make an appropriate response. Sensitivity to each other's feelings involves more than just hearing the words that are spoken. Behaviors and body language often convey deeper meanings and need to be considered as well.

Developing effective communication includes finding ways to handle disagreements and conflict. Some couples think they are protecting their relationship by overlooking differences, but more likely the opposite is true. Instead of protecting a relationship, ignoring differences can make it more superficial and fragile. Facing differences and working them through in most cases strengthens the relationship and deepens intimacy. In addition to making decisions and solving problems together, couples need to know how to repair their relationship when it has been damaged. (Couple's Manual, Sections 4.1-4.3, 2.3)

Providing the Necessities of Life

Finding and maintaining a place to live is a primary concern. Whether it is in a small one-room rented apartment or a large, fully furnished house, the couple's task is to make a *home* for themselves. Finding and furnishing a new residence requires many joint decisions. Compromise is often necessary, perhaps in the location of the house or in the choice of furnishings. One or both of the partners may have to be satisfied with less than what they were accustomed to while growing up.

The necessities of life also include such items as food, clothing, medical care, and transportation. Providing these, too, will call for joint decision-making and compromise. The couple must learn to work together as a team, respecting each other's individual tastes, considering each other's needs, and making choices that reflect their values and goals in life. These decisions provide an excellent opportunity for practicing the communication and conflict-management skills they have been taught. (Couple's Manual, Section 3.1)

Managing Finances

Couples need to develop mutually acceptable ways to earn and spend their money and satisfactory methods for managing their resources. The vocational and career goals of both partners must be given equal consideration, necessitating adjustments in regard to schedules, transportation, household tasks, and where they will live. Feelings about and expectations in regard to these adjustments, which depend on their values and goals, should be fully explored. What if one partner's work requires a move to another city? Does the one with the larger income deserve greater consideration? What adjustments will have to be made by each partner when the couple has children?

Values and goals also play a vital role in a couple's decisions about spending. The principles of Christian stewardship promote awareness of the world's limited resources and advocate for simplified living; but many persons assume that if they have money, they might as well spend it. Couples need to work through any values differences and learn to make decisions together, functioning as a team. Marriage also requires more thought for the future, perhaps in the form of savings and insurance. A mutually agreed-upon budget will help couples meet their goals by guiding their spending and by providing a basis for reviewing their cash flow on a regular basis. Early in their life together, a couple may find they need to make frequent adjustments to their spending plan due to expenses they had not previously considered. If they plan to have children, they will be wise to learn to live on a lower-than-necessary standard of living in preparation for a time of less income and increased expenses.

Among items often overlooked in early attempts at budgeting are gifts, recreation, savings, and individual allowances. Young couples will want to buy wedding and baby gifts for their peers, in addition to the expense of gifts for their combined extended families. Some couples think they will not need much money for recreation once they are married, but it is important for them to set aside funds for recreational and educational activities that they enjoy and that will strengthen their companionship. Medical insurance is critically important, and the couple may need to investigate and compare policies available through their jobs or other sources. They may also need to be encouraged to set aside a percentage of their income to save for short-term emergencies and long-term goals. Both partners should have some spending money that they do not have to account for with each other. You may also suggest that they practice Christian stewardship by setting aside a portion of their income for helping others through the church and charitable organizations. (Couple's Manual, Section 3.2)

Establishing Husband and Wife Roles

In the past, husband and wife roles were more clearly defined, but today couples have to decide for themselves who is responsible for what. These changing patterns and this new freedom can create confusion and conflict. Men and women frequently are not even aware of underlying feelings carried over from experiences in their families of origin. Couples may need help expressing their feelings and learning to respect each other's personal preferences and abilities as they work out their responsibilities together. (Couple's Manual, Sections 1.3, 2.1, and Explore 3.1 A)

Meeting Personal Needs

Each individual brings to marriage psychological and emotional needs requiring attention and nurture from the other. Most of us need to be affirmed as persons of worth and to have our self-esteem fed and strengthened in healthy ways. Our needs for respect and privacy are important as well. Persons need and rightfully expect to experience affection, fellowship, and companionship in marriage. Some of that may be fulfilled through a couple's sexual relationship, but not all. (Couple's Manual, Section 3.3)

It may take some experimenting and adjustment to find a good balance between intimacy and distance, companionship and privacy, a sense of belonging and a sense of autonomy. Changing life circumstances affect this balance, challenging couples to renegotiate their relationships from time to time. Effective communication and conflict-resolution skills are critical for finding ways to meet personal needs while balancing family life and careers and community involvement. (Couple's Manual, Section 3.5)

Planning for Children

Another task for couples is decision-making in regard to having children. Today many couples decide not to become parents. However, if they plan to have children they need to talk together about how many, how soon, and how far apart. Most couples find it best to give themselves time to adjust to each other before they take on the responsibility of adjusting to a child. Some couples, on the other hand, already have children, either from previous marriages or from their own relationship. Occasionally couples have already taken on responsibility for someone else's children, perhaps those of a sibling or close friend.

Ideally, parenthood is seen as a Christian vocation. This means it is entered into in response to God's call to join in the creative process, bringing new children into the world and helping them grow to full maturity as persons in Christ. Planning for children involves careful consideration of the physical and emotional health of both parents, their educational and vocational plans, their financial situation, and personal preferences. If both partners are working, plans should be made for child care expenses or loss of income if one becomes a full-time parent or both shift to part-time work. If a couple waits for perfect conditions, however, they may never have children!

Adequate medical advice regarding birth control is important to every couple, but more so to couples in special circumstances. Those who still need to complete their education or find work with adequate pay must feel secure about their method of birth control in order to enjoy sexual relations without fear of an unplanned pregnancy. You might inquire about how they feel about the advice they have received from their physician or elsewhere. You may also need to reassure them about the morality of contraception and the church's stand on birth control.[1] Every child deserves to be wanted and planned for as a gift from God. Therefore couples should get the best medical advice available and find a family planning method suited to their needs. An unplanned pregnancy can be a real crisis in the life of a couple, especially if they are still struggling to get started in life together. But if such a pregnancy does occur, they should know that their pastor and their church family are available to help them adjust to the new situation in the most constructive manner possible. (Couple's Manual, Section 3.4)

Adjusting to Relatives

Many couples feel that only the husband and wife are getting married and that they do not need to concern themselves with their immediate families, especially not with more distant relatives. In fact, two whole families come into a new relationship through marriage. The nature of this relationship depends on how much closeness there is within each family of origin.

Some couples may have difficulty establishing independence from their parents. They may need your support in maintaining the primacy of their own marriage as a new unit. One or both persons may still be too dependent on the parents or may feel guilty about moving away from the parental home, especially when some emotional or financial need is involved. Such separation is necessary, however, if the new marriage is to have a life of its own. This does not mean that couples should cut themselves off from their parental families, but rather that they will have to find new ways of relating to relatives that will not weaken the marital bond.

The family systems theory discussed in Edwin H. Friedman's *Generation to Generation* suggests that our anxieties and conflicts are not caused so much by the unique make-up of our personalities, but by our "relational networks." It is misleading, he asserts, to consider a marriage in isolation from the extended families of the couple. Personal emotional health and marriage relationships can be improved then, when individuals work through unresolved issues with their families of origin.[2] This task is not likely to be accomplished quickly, but may, in fact, take many years. (Couple's Manual, Section 1.2 and also Explore 3.4F in Section 3.4)

Making and Keeping Friends

Newly married couples are faced with many adjustments in regard to friends and associates. You can help them face this task realistically in four specific ways.

First, some couples think they do not need any friends after they are married. They may be so much in love and so absorbed in their relationship that they believe they need only each other. Anticipating that two people can completely meet all of each other's needs is expecting too much of each other and of marriage. It is fine for the couple to be alone for a while, but soon after the honeymoon they need to reconnect with others.

A second mistake some couples make is thinking that friendships take care of themselves, that they do not need to do anything to initiate or maintain them. Social activities with friends may develop easily and naturally before marriage, but after the wedding more deliberate effort will probably be required. Marriage moves the couple into a different world. They will have to take responsibility for the development and nurturing of friendships, both with other couples and with individual or single friends as well.

Third, a couple must decide which of their old friends they want to keep. Most couples bring to marriage three sets of friends: hers, his, and theirs. Each individual probably has some friends who are not very well known to the other. These friendships may create some tensions after marriage, especially if one person does not like certain of the other's friends. Maintaining friendships with members of the opposite sex, especially if they are still single, can be threatening to one's marriage partner. Both husband and wife have to work together to find an agreeable way of establishing boundaries and maintaining the friendships they both want to keep. (Couple's Manual, Explore 3.4G)

Fourth, making new friends is an important part of establishing a couple identity. New friends may be other newly married couples, or they may include persons of a different age group. In either case, new friendships can be formed around interests and activities that the couples enjoy or in which they find meaning. Whether or not entertaining is expected of them because of their jobs, couples can also develop friendships with colleagues where they work. You may be able to help a new couple find a church school class or couples' fellowship group in your church or community. Of if they are moving to a new community, you may be able to help them connect with a congenial group by contacting the pastor of a church in the community to which they are going.

Taking Part in Community Life

The final developmental task for newlyweds, and one that is often overlooked, is finding a place for themselves in various community activities, organizations, or movements. Although the focus is often local, these may include state, national, and world interests. Some couples may need encouragement to realize that they are part of the larger community and that they have an opportunity to contribute to the shaping of culture and events. Others may have a keen sense of responsibility, but need help in making their influence effective. They might be opposed to many things happening in their community, nation, and world, but not certain about how they can work toward improving conditions. Some become disillusioned very quickly, perhaps because of the hypocrisy and often outright dishonesty they discover among organizations or people they formerly respected. They may also become disillusioned because of their unrealistic expectations for immediate change.

You can help couples find their place within church and community organizations that work for good, encouraging them not to be overwhelmed and discouraged by difficulties and disappointments they encounter. Sometimes, especially for newcomers, you will be able to provide contacts for community involvement that will enrich and strengthen their relationship and provide opportunities for them to contribute to the general good. Primarily, of course, this task, like all the others, is the responsibility of the couple; as their pastor, however, you can alert them to the task and inspire them to work on it. (Couple's Manual, Section 2.2)

8

MENTOR COUPLES

"... surrounded by so great a cloud of witnesses..." (Hebrews 12:1).

Even ministers who love to do premarital counseling would be wise to consider establishing a mentor couples program. Mentor couples, sometimes called sponsor couples, offer a unique peer relationship and a couple-to-couple dynamic of support that no pastor can provide by himself or herself. Engaged couples must meet with the pastor to discuss details of the wedding service and usually to deal with some other topics, but mentor couples can give more time to relationship-building activities. Meeting with a well-trained mentor couple and with a caring and competent minister provides engaged couples with a comprehensive marriage preparation program. Newlyweds in your congregation who were married elsewhere and did not participate in your marriage preparation program would also benefit from a mentor couple relationship at least through their first year or two of marriage.

A church needs to clarify its position in regard to how confidential the mentoring sessions will be. In some cases mentor couples share with the pastor who is marrying the couple the results of the premarital inventories they use and what issues they are addressing in their mentoring sessions. The mentorees should know if this is the case from the beginning, and they should also be assured that personal information will not otherwise be shared without their permission. However, mentor couples who have serious concerns about their partner couple, such as suspicion of abuse, should bring those

matters to the pastor or mentoring coordinator for assistance with making an appropriate referral.

What Mentor Couples Do

Mentor couples in marriage preparation ministries serve as lay volunteers, sharing information, facilitating discussion, and offering encouragement to engaged couples and newlyweds. Other mentor couples specialize in ministries to couples in later stages of marriage and to those with special needs, such as new parents, parents of teens, or couples facing various transitions and crises. In either case, mentor couples do not try to function as counselors or therapists, but offer peer-level caring and sharing. Although the focus of this chapter is on mentoring engaged and newlywed couples, some of these ideas would apply as well in other types of mentoring programs. As you discover couples with various gifts and experiences willing to serve in this way, your mentoring program can expand to serve a variety of needs. See Chapter 10 for more information about ministries to couples who have been married for a while and to those who are in crisis.

Mentor couples working with engaged and newlywed couples explore in depth a variety of issues: marriage goals and expectations, communication, conflict resolution, financial planning, household roles, faith issues, and spiritual practices. They reinforce the strengths of the couples with whom they work, while modeling and teaching the communication skills needed for enduring, fulfilling relationships. Mentor couples might explain to couples how participating in a premarital chastity covenant can deepen and strengthen their relationship, inviting them to make such a commitment. A mentor couple usually meets privately with the engaged or newlywed couple assigned to them, but may also participate in planning and leading group sessions such as seminars on communication, conflict management, or financial planning. They also participate in regular mentoring team meetings for ongoing training and sharing with other mentor couples. (See Appendix II for a sample mentoring covenant and Appendix III for suggestions for a liturgy to involve mentor couples in wedding ceremonies.)

The pastor or marriage ministry planning team usually recommends a minimum number of sessions and specific procedures for mentoring, which may include:

- using the GROWING LOVE IN CHRISTIAN MARRIAGE Couple's Manual or similar resource, such as Marriage Mentoring: Twelve Conversations (See Resources);
- administrating and interpreting a premarital inventory;
- discussing topics such as the "Tasks of Marriage" (Chapter 7).

How Mentoring Sessions Might Be Structured

Information from the Wedding Information form in the Couple's Manual helps a mentor couple make contact and schedule sessions with their partner couple. Although expectations may vary from place to place and even within a church community, according to the resources available and the needs and interests of those who participate, the following outline offers some idea of what might take place when a mentor couple meets with an engaged or newlywed couple. This outline assumes a minimum commitment of three sessions.

Mentoring Session One

The mentor couple might begin by asking their partner couple to tell about how they met, what attracted them to each other, how their relationship developed, when they decided to marry, and what plans they have made for the wedding and their life together. A newlywed couple might be invited to bring along their wedding pictures. The mentor couple would share some of their own story, as well. By demonstrating personal interest in their mentorees and by openly sharing about their own relationship, the mentor couple begins to build a supportive relationship, which is the most powerful element of the mentoring program.

The mentor couple will want to be sure the partner couple understands how the mentoring program works and what they might expect. (See Appendix II for a sample covenant statement designed to clarify expectations.) Confidentiality must be discussed, as well as how often the couples will meet. If a premarital inventory is administered, the mentor couple should explain how it will be used and to what extent, if any, the pastor will be involved in processing their responses. (See Chapter 4 for information about administering such inventories.) If the couple is new to the congregation and/or community, the mentor couple may also inform them about other available sources of support and fellowship.

Mentoring Session Two

Goals for mentoring should be developed jointly by the two couples, either by reviewing the results of a premarital inventory or through a discussion process. If no inventory has been used, or if the pastor intends to use such an instrument with the couple, the mentors might begin by asking what characteristics the mentorees want to have in their marriage and what characteristics they wish to avoid. While looking through the GROWING LOVE IN CHRISTIAN MARRIAGE Couple's Manual together, the mentors can ask the mentorees which topics interest them most. Another approach would be to use a "Tasks of Marriage" list, as discussed in Chapter 7. The mentor couple could identify areas that have been strengths and/or a struggle for them, emphasizing experiences and resources that have helped them grow. They might then ask the mentorees to identify areas they think are strengths in their own relationship and areas in which they would like to improve. Beginning to share around some of these indicated interests will help build the couple's confidence in and commitment to the mentoring process.

Mentoring Session Three and Beyond

During the third session, the two couples continue to work on issues that have been raised by the premarital inventory, the Couple's Manual, or the "Tasks of Marriage" list. At some point in this session, the mentorees should be asked to assess their progress and continuing needs so that plans can be made for future meetings. Mentoring programs often encourage an ongoing relationship to continue for at least two years. Mentor couples may attend the weddings of engaged couples they have worked with, invite them over for dinner or dessert, and drop them notes or cards on their anniversaries or other important occasions.[1] Some churches involve mentor couples in the wedding ceremony itself (Appendix III).

However your program is structured, mentor couples should:

- Talk enthusiastically about the positive aspects of marriage.
- Challenge engaged couples to set and pursue goals for their relationship.
- Use anecdotes from their own marriage history to illustrate important points and to encourage the engaged couple.
- Acknowledge that struggles are a normal part of marriage, and help couples learn effective ways to talk about and deal with them.
- Empathize with the engaged couple while supporting and nurturing their progress.
- Demonstrate openness to learning from the engaged couple, especially about how to be more effective mentors.
- Go easy with advice-giving. Listen, listen, listen!

Selecting and Recruiting Mentor Couples

Since mentor couples serve as role models and will be seen as extensions of the minister and of the church itself, you will want to select couples who demonstrate strong faith, who have been married for at least five years, and who appear to be in growing, healthy relationships. Administering one of the relationship inventories may help identify any potential relationship problems that might impact a couple's effectiveness as a mentor and can also give them a change to experience whatever tools they will be using (see Resources.) When possible, recruit a mix of different couple types: those of various ages and numbers of years married, some in remarriages, those with and without children, and some with differences in religious background and ethnic heritage. Look for couples with a variety of experiences and interests so that you can match up couples with enough commonalities to help establish rapport and empathy. You will want to devise a form on which prospective mentor couples can indicate their professional or vocational roles, hobbies, interests, and other relevant factors that will help you make viable mentoring assignments.

Make sure that a prospective mentor couple has:

- time to commit to the ministry without neglecting their own family;
- spiritual gifts of mercy, teaching, service, and administration;
- a healthy Christian lifestyle;
- good communication skills and habits;
- a positive attitude;
- a desire to serve together in ministry;
- the ability to work well as a team;
- the desire to strengthen, enrich, and learn more about their own marriage.

Mentor couples should understand that taking part in this ministry involves participation in an intensive training program using the same study materials they will later use with their mentorees. They should not expect to use the program as a showcase for their own marriage or as a platform for preaching. Persons not suited to serve as mentor couples include those who believe they have a perfect marriage, those who tend to be controlling or aggressive or judgmental, those who have any history of physical or emotional abuse in their own marriage, or those who suffer from alcoholism or other addictions. Persons in recovery from such problems, however, might be trained to mentor other couples needing help in that area.

Announce the training sessions during Sunday school classes and in various small groups, and during regular worship services, in the bulletin and in the church newsletter. Schedule a special orientation meeting during which potential mentor couples can learn about how the program functions and what the training entails. Include in such a meeting a testimonial from someone who has been through the program. You might also provide for such testimonials during worship and set up a booth where persons can ask questions after services during the weeks before training begins. Provide brochures and sample materials for interested persons to look over and take home for more thorough consideration. Pray for God to direct to mentor couple training people who belong there!

Program Costs

Churches could begin a mentor couple ministry with a carefully managed budget of several hundred dollars. Some may want to invest more funding in order to hire paid staff. Basic expenses include:

- Workbooks or other resources for couples to be mentored. A fee may be charged to cover this cost, but scholarships should be available for those who can't afford to pay.
- Relationship inventories, such as that in the GROWING LOVE IN CHRISTIAN MARRIAGE Couple's Manual, PREPARE/ENRICH or FOCCUS (See Resources).
- Additional resources, such as copies of worksheets and other handouts.
- Training materials for mentor couples. The church may cover the cost of workbooks and training manuals for each mentor couple, or the mentor couples could pay for their own.
- Envelopes, cards, and postage for program evaluations, six-month anniversary follow-up greeting cards, and other program-related materials.
- Refreshments for periodic social activities, monthly mentoring team meetings, and services for commissioning newly-trained mentor couples.

Leadership Team

The key to the success of a mentor couple program is the support of the pastor or senior minister. If the pastor or senior minister embraces this lay ministry both intellectually and practically, the members of the congregation will take his or her lead.

A minister, licensed professional counselor, social worker, family life educator, marriage and family therapist, or other person with appropriate leadership and organization skills could serve effectively as coordinator of this program. This person may be paid or may serve as a volunteer. Capable lay people can be recruited to function as part of the leadership team to share responsibility for ongoing management of the program.

Specific tasks for the leadership team include:

- recruiting mentor couples for training;
- designing the curriculum for training mentor couples;
- selecting speakers and discussion leaders with particular areas of expertise to participate in training sessions;
- selecting and/or developing appropriate materials;
- planning for ongoing supervision and continuing education of mentor couples, perhaps through regular monthly meetings;
- assigning a suitable mentor couple to each newly referred couple as promptly as possible;
- assisting in referrals of mentoree couples to appropriate professionals when needed;
- compiling annual reports based on evaluations by participating engaged and newlywed couples.

Training Mentor Couples

Mentor couples need solid training in using appropriate materials and in the interpersonal skills they will demonstrate and teach. Mentor couples should know how to facilitate the engaged or newlywed couple's learning process rather than preach to or attempt to control them. Training can be offered as a series of weekly evening sessions or for longer blocks of time on weekends. Trainees should commit to attend all sessions with the understanding that each person may miss no more than a limited number of sessions. Training classes of at least four and up to ten mentor couples provide the best group dynamics. Trainees should also be encouraged to participate in marriage enrichment events and to read books from the list provided in the Resources section in the Growing Love in Christian Marriage Couple's Manual and in this pastor's manual.

Mentor couple training should include ample use of experiential activities, role-play, and hands-on practice. Such activities, especially if built around various situations that may actually arise while working with their partner couples, help mentor couples feel more comfortable and confident. A comprehensive training program might include.

1. Basic information

- the purpose and structure of the program;
- role distinctions for minister, counselor, and mentor couples;
- the importance of confidentiality;
- forms and procedures for assignments, initial contacts, recordkeeping, and evaluation.

2. Relationship building for mentor couples

- Reading, discussion, and exercises related to topics suggested by whatever relationship inventory they take.
- activities from workbooks that the engaged/newlywed couples will use or other couple communication exercises (See Resources).

3. Skill development

- listening;
- working as a team;
- using the workbook material or other exercises;
- dealing with challenges (such as one partner doing all the talking);
- avoiding the dangers of triangulation and taking sides;
- deciding when to refer a couple for professional help.

An important aspect of mentoring other couples is nurturing personal and couple spiritual growth. An authentic, personal style of faith sharing will have much more impact than a preachy, judgmental style. Mentor couples will vary, as will the mentorees, in their degree of comfort with religious language. During initial training and in the regular mentoring team meetings, you can encourage the mentors to find ways to speak naturally of their faith and how they understand God to be at work in their lives. You will also want to encourage their sensitivity to couples with different religious experiences and different cultural or ethnic backgrounds. If you use materials that are not biblically based, you can help mentor couples select relevant Scripture passages and plan effective and appropriate ways to incorporate them into their mentoring sessions. Mentor couples may also need guidance and practice in regard to praying for and with their mentorees.

If mentor couples are to administer and interpret any or all of a relationship inventory, such as the one at the back of the Growing Love in Christian Marriage Couple's Manual (or PREPARE or FOCCUS), training should include how to introduce and administer the forms to couples and how to interpret and present the results. If you use any other materials in addition to the above inventories, mentor couples may need training in their administration and interpretation, as well.

Listening Skills

Listening skills training can help persons learn to set aside judgmental attitudes in order to increase understanding, build relationships, promote respect, and convey caring. Good listening requires putting your own thoughts and concerns on hold and letting another tell his or her full story, without interference from you. The following five skills improve one's ability to listen:

- Attending—Look at the speaker, stop any distracting activity, and listen, observing nonverbal cues and noticing whether the speaker is sharing thoughts, ideas, feelings, wants, or actions.
- Acknowledging—Let the speaker know that you are following what he or she is saying. Give nonverbal and verbal feedback to express acceptance, understanding, and empathy. "You seem excited (concerned, etc.)."
- Inviting—Say or do something to encourage the speaker to continue. Keep this general and open-ended so that the speaker will feel free to say what he or she wants to say. "Tell me more about that," "I'd like to hear more. . . ."

- Summarizing—Repeat in your own words what you think the speaker said and ask for confirmation or clarification of your summary.
- Asking—To clarify unclear messages, begin with sensory data and use open-ended questions that require something other than a yes-or-no or either-or response. "You sound angry. What's up?" or "You're quiet this evening. How are you feeling?" Avoid asking "why" questions, which make the other feel challenged, blamed, or put on the defensive.[2]

Mentor couples should be helped to identify strengths in their listening habits, uncover areas where they need to improve, and practice effective listening skills. Through good listening they can convey God's love and come to a better understanding of their mentorees, while at the same time serving as role models for them. (See also the Couple's Manual, Section 4.1)

Teamwork Training

Learning to work effectively as a team is an important aspect of mentor couple training. The unique combination of skills and experience a husband and wife bring to their "couple-to-couple" ministry affords an entirely different dynamic from that of a clergy person or therapist working alone. A husband and wife team can offer individual perspectives on male/female roles in marriage, share their unique gifts, suggest alternative viewpoints on important issues, and observe reactions and feelings through two pairs of eyes and ears.

Mentor couples should decide before each session who will "lead" and who will be the "support" person. Both roles are equally important. One spouse may prefer to lead for particular topics or workbook chapters, or one may prefer always—or usually—to take one role rather than the other.

The lead spouse usually:

- focuses more on discussion content;
- makes sure that all the material gets covered;
- asks most of the questions;
- talks more than the support spouse;
- keeps everyone on task.

The support spouse usually:

- focuses more on feelings and process;
- observes nonverbal communication;
- asks questions about feelings when they are not obvious;
- helps to regulate the mood (by lightening things up, for example);
- shares observations when appropriate;
- may rescue the lead spouse when asked.

Both spouses are vital members of the team. Mentor couples should always pray before, during, and after mentoring sessions and refrain from interrupting or embarrassing each other. Checking in with each other in the course of mentoring sessions, however, by sharing feelings and making suggestions in a positive manner allows them to own their humanness and model effective communication.

Program Supervision

Program supervision, critical for maintaining the effectiveness of the mentoring program, involves staying in touch with the mentor couples and keeping them motivated. Ongoing training and supervision is vital for quality control. Regular meetings, perhaps once a month, allow mentor couples to share experiences and do problem solving with each other in a supportive setting. Mentor team meetings usually focus on the skills of the mentor couples, not the specific issues being addressed with their mentorees. If personal information is revealed, this group should be reminded to protect the couple's privacy and honor the confidentiality of the mentoring relationship. These meetings also provide a forum for continuing education and for reinforcement of skills already learned.

Mentoring team meetings should include:

- prayer, motivational input, and encouragement;
- updates on referrals and assignments;
- communication of essential information;
- discussion of topics related to marriage and mentoring;
- opportunities for progress reports and feedback;
- suggestions for dealing with various problems that might arise;
- ongoing training and skills practice.

Materials for discussion and review can be found in the Couple's Manual, in books on the reading lists in this manual, and in other resources listed in the Resources section. Mentoring team meetings might also feature panel discussions with married couples who have been mentored through the program, refresher courses on interpreting the relationship inventory, or discussions with the minister or other resource persons about marital issues, such as cohabitation, divorce, and remarriage.

Another important aspect of regular meetings is the opportunity for mentor couples to connect and share with each other, to experience mutual support, and to realize that they belong to a vital ministry. Schedule time for mentor couples to get better acquainted and have fun with each other. Informal potluck dinners, picnics, game nights, theme parties (such as Christmas or Valentine's Day), and other activities might also include the families of mentor couples. Thoughtful tokens of appreciation, such as a couple-oriented devotional book, Christmas ornament, or a gift certificate, assure mentor couples that their ministry is recognized and valued.

Program Evaluation

In order to determine the strengths of your program and the areas needing improvement, you need to obtain feedback from the mentor couples about their training and ongoing supervision and from the couples with whom they work.

The Marriage Preparation Evaluation Form at the back of this manual may be copied or modified to obtain feedback from couples on all aspects of their marriage preparation. An evaluation form for mentor couples might ask the following questions.

- How well have you been helped to understand your role as a mentor couple?
- To what extent have you been allowed to express your thoughts and feelings?
- To what extent has the leadership team provided positive role models?
- How well equipped do you feel to administer and interpret relationship inventory materials?
- To what extent do you feel you have learned to be better communicators and listeners?
- To what extent do you feel equipped to facilitate discussions using the Couple's Manual or other resource? Using the "Tasks of Marriage?"
- To what extent do you feel equipped to deal with unanticipated issues?
- In what ways do you feel you have grown as a couple through this ministry?

Mentor couples should also be encouraged to make suggestions for further training and supervision or for ways to improve the program in general. Although successful mentoring programs require careful planning, training, and ongoing supervision, trained lay couples can greatly enhance your marriage preparation ministry. Mentor couples can also help you serve couples who have been married for a while and those in special situations. In most local churches, willing, interested, and gifted couples are just waiting to be invited to serve by helping other couples build strong, fulfilling marriages. Mentor couple programs reflect good stewardship of resources, time, and energy.

9

MARRIAGE PREPARATION
IN GROUPS

"For where two or three are gathered in my name, I am there among them"
(Matthew 18:20).

Group experiences can add to the effectiveness of your marriage preparation ministry. Such sessions do not replace the premarital counseling you do with each couple, but supplement and complement your private meetings with them. You can work on many of the tasks of marriage preparation while meeting with groups of engaged couples and efficiently fulfill the requirements of a community marriage agreement (Chapter 10). Three hours of private sessions and twelve hours of group activities, for example, could meet a requirement of fifteen hours of directed marriage preparation activity. Even if you have only four couples in your group, twelve hours of group time would save thirty-six hours of private couple meeting time. You might schedule a series of evening meetings, perhaps with refreshments or a light supper, or you could meet for a longer time block on two or three Saturdays. In fact, you do not necessarily have to lead or participate in all the group sessions. You can involve other professionals or lay persons within your congregation or parish who have appropriate expertise and training. Materials for use with groups are listed in the Resources section of this manual along with organizations providing leadership and leadership training.

Group sessions also bring dynamics to marriage preparation quite different from those experienced in private counseling sessions with you:

- In groups, couples can experience a sense of trust in the context of Christian community. As they open themselves to each other and to the group, they may become more aware of God's love and the power of the Holy Spirit to help them reach their potential.
- The group experience helps break "the marital taboo," the common belief that couples should not talk with anyone else about what goes on in their relationship. Couples discover that they are not alone in their struggles and that they can learn from each other.
- In group settings, dynamic interactions encourage couples to try new ways of relating and to evaluate their expectations and behaviors more realistically.
- Group activities provide fun and fellowship, helping couples build supportive peer relationships.

In group experiences, you want to enhance learning by using the best possible methods. We recall little of what we hear and only somewhat more of what we see, remembering best that which we actually experience. Consequently you want to provide opportunities for the couples to participate as much as possible. You can invite the group to brainstorm lists to be posted on newsprint, such as their hopes and concerns in regard to marriage. You can have couples talk with each other privately or in small groups. One couple can coach another through a specific communication or problem-solving procedure (keeping them in the process without getting involved in their issue). In the "fishbowl" technique, men silently observe women discuss a marital issue (and vice versa). You can also use nonverbal techniques such as making collages, drawing pictures, or miming. Other creative activities include reacting to films or videotapes, role-playing marital discussions, and couples talking knee-to-knee. Affirmation exercises strengthen a couple's bond, and worship experiences can both challenge and inspire.

Five possible approaches for group marriage preparation are described below, followed by discussion of other options you might consider.

GROWING LOVE IN CHRISTIAN MARRIAGE Groups

The material in the GROWING LOVE IN CHRISTIAN MARRIAGE Couple's Manual can easily be adapted for use by groups. Leadership should be given by couples, perhaps those trained through mentor couple programs or marriage enrichment experiences, so that they can model the use of the Explore activities. The workbook material could provide the framework for a series of ten evening sessions or for a weekly church school class. Topics could be combined for half-day, full-day, or weekend events as well. Depending on the needs of the participating couples, you may want to give more time to some of the topics. Regardless of the schedule, providing a time and place for engaging in the Explore activities, followed by opportunities for couples to share reactions and insights with each other, will greatly enhance what they gain from the material. The following outline may be adapted to fit the needs of your engaged and newlywed couples.[1] Section references in parentheses are to the GROWING LOVE IN CHRISTIAN MARRIAGE Couple's Manual.

Session 1: Marriage as a Lifetime Journey
(Perspectives on Marriage and Theme One)

This session focuses on the meaning of marriage as expressed through the wedding service. In addition to presentation and discussion of the material on these pages, the leader couples should model

the Explore exercises (A, B, 1) in the group setting and then give the participating couples time to do the same. This would also be a good opportunity to present an overview of marriage ministry in your congregation or parish.

Session 2: What Do We Bring to Our Marriage?
(Sections 1.1-1.2)

Each individual brings to marriage a set of personal characteristics, habits, and skills. In addition, each comes from a unique family-of-origin experience, with its particular relationship dynamics. Persons who have been married before have been shaped by that experience as well. In addition to the Explore exercises in this section, skits and role-plays could be used to open up discussion about interpersonal issues in a humorous way. Each person could be asked to prepare a genogram (Explore 1.2B) or family tree including their own family of origin and that of their parents and grandparents. This activity can help to surface information and observations about recurring patterns in family relationships, helping couples make considered decisions about how they will relate with each other and with their respective families.

Session 3: What Are Our Expectations?
(Sections 1:3-1.4)

Comparing assumptions, expectations, and goals helps couples discover common values and anticipate possible conflicts. Leader couples can share their own experiences of modifying expectations and goals over the years and of learning to cope with their differences and conflicts.

Session 4: How Do We Communicate?
(Section 4.1)

During this session, participant couples will learn about and practice effective communication skills: how to send a message without putting the other person on the defensive and how to hear and understand what the other person is saying. These skills should be reviewed and reinforced throughout the remaining sessions.

Session 5: Dealing With Change (Sections 4.2-4.3)

With continuing emphasis on effective communication, this session addresses problem solving and conflict resolution. Skits by leader couples, role-plays, and excerpts from movies can be used to illustrate common couple dynamics. Couples will benefit from the opportunity to practice the process in Section 4.3 with coaching and feedback from the rest of the group.

Session 6: Sexual Intimacy (Section 3.3)

This session considers how affection, intimacy, and sexual expression can enrich and nurture marriage. The Explore activities in this material provide an opportunity for couples to learn to talk comfortably about their intimate feelings and relationship. Invite a physician or trained sexuality educator to present current information and answer questions.

Session 7: Money, Possessions, and Work (Sections 3.1, 3.2, and 3.5)

In this material, finances and career issues are presented from a Christian stewardship perspective. Leader couples may describe how they live out their values through their careers and money management. This session can also consider stewardship of health and the effect of work schedules and demands on marriage and family life.

Session 8: Caring for Others: Children, Relatives, Friends (Section 3.4)

This session focuses on parenting and on other relationships that impact marriage. Stepfamily issues may be addressed here or in additional sessions for couples in which one or both of the partners already have children.

Session 9: Connections (Section 2.2)

This session provides opportunities to consider leisure activities, church involvement, and community/world concerns.

Session 10: Looking Ahead (Sections 2.1, 2.3, 2.4)

Marriage is a lifelong journey for growing in love. The activities in this session encourage a long-range view and a healthy anticipation of life stages and transitions. This might also be an appropriate time to consider serious problems, such as addictions, that can threaten marriage, and to discuss how to determine when couples need professional help.

Couple Communication Workshops

A Couple Communication Workshop brings together a small group of couples under the guidance of trained and experienced leader couples. These workshops are designed to help participants grow in understanding themselves and each other and discover how improved communication can enrich their relationship. Such a workshop might be scheduled for engaged couples, newlyweds, or for mixed groups of both. Couples become aware of how they have been relating, discover strengths and weaknesses in their relationships, and decide on new directions for future growth. A Couple Communication Workshop is not therapy; nor is it a substitute for premarital counseling. It does, however, prevent problems by preparing couples to face differences constructively when they do arise.

A Couple Communication Workshop may be scheduled as a weekend retreat, on two separate Saturdays (9:00 a.m. to 9:00 p.m.), on evenings over a period of six or more weeks, or some combination of the above options. Weekly sessions afford couples time to practice skills between sessions, but it is sometimes difficult to ensure consistent attendance.

Topics explored include:

• looking at our relationship now;
• improving communication;
• finding sexual fulfillment in marriage;
• considering roles and expectations;
• enhancing intimacy and identity;
• expressing positive and negative feelings;
• facing conflicts constructively;
• deepening our spiritual life;
• setting goals for growth.

The Couple Communication Workshop requires trained leadership and should not be attempted without it. One source of such training is Better Marriages, formerly know as the Association for Couples in Marriage Enrichment. You can call the international office or check the website to find out if there are trained leader couples in your area or if a leadership training workshop is scheduled that would be convenient for you or someone in your church or parish. Family Dynamics Institute also offers a similar program. If you contact local counseling centers in your community, you might find other resource persons equipped to lead such an experience. Most smaller churches would do well to sponsor such an event cooperatively with other churches in order to recruit an adequate number of participant couples.

Premarital Marriage Seminars

You can no doubt find within your congregation, or at least within your community, resource persons who could share helpful information on specific topics for young couples. Here are several possibilities for evening or weekend seminars:

- "What Is Marriage All About?" A minister trained in family life education could explore the meaning of marriage as a covenant relationship and a Christian vocation.
- "Our Bodies/Ourselves" A medical doctor could present information about the physical aspects of the marriage relationship, family planning, and general health.
- "What Does the Law Say?" A lawyer could discuss legal issues related to marriage, such as income tax, property, insurance, and wills.
- "Being Me and Being Married" A psychotherapist could help couples look at the personal and emotional adjustments involved in marriage.
- "And What Does It Cost?" A home economist and/or financial planner could focus on decisions regarding earning and spending, budgeting, and planning for the future.

These and other topics can be presented as a series or as separate events for engaged couples, newlyweds, or for mixed groups of both. Such programs also provide a time of fellowship for the participating couples and an opportunity for them to establish new friendships with others in their peer group.

Sharing Groups

A more informal approach would be to invite several engaged couples who are preparing for marriage to meet with several married couples of different ages and life stages who are open to sharing about their marriage experience. You might find married couples who have participated in marriage enrichment or Marriage Encounter or mentor couple training who would be willing to share in such a setting. One pastor convened such a group, initially for two sessions, inviting the younger couples to ask the married couples anything about their marriages they wanted to. The married couples were not to give advice, but they were to share their stories and tell about what they had learned. Although the married couples were told they could "pass" on any questions they preferred not to answer, this never happened. During the second session, after responding to the questions that were asked of them, the married couples asked if they could question the engaged couples about their relationships. The engaged couples agreed, and there followed a free exchange in which all the couples learned from one another. At the end of the evening, one of the engaged persons remarked to the married couples, "You caused us to ask questions we didn't even know we had." Another asked if they could meet again, which they did.

The best way to prepare to lead this kind of informal group is to get involved in a marital growth group yourself. If you have couples who have had experience with the Better Marriages or with Marriage Encounter, bring them together as a marital growth group. Working on the growing areas in their own relationships in a group setting will help them become more comfortable about meeting in sharing groups with engaged couples.

Engaged Encounter

Engaged Encounter is a weekend experience designed to help couples prepare for marriage. A positive and personal experience, the weekend gives couples the opportunity for private reflection and discussion of their dreams, ambitions, and attitudes.

During the weekend three married couples, including some clergy, give presentations on different topics, modeling effective communication of feelings. After each presentation, participants have private time to reflect on their own thoughts and feelings, followed by private couple time for sharing. This experience deepens the couple's awareness of each other's thoughts, feelings, and attitudes as they prepare together for the covenant of marriage.

The Engaged Encounter Weekend experience, which provides about twenty hours of direct contact time for couples, is designed to be a supplement to, not a substitute for the pastor's personal premarital counseling. Couples of all ages, including those entering second marriages, will find the weekend beneficial and nonthreatening. A wide variety of subjects are presented, giving each engaged couple freedom to explore the areas important to them. Engaged Encounter—United Methodist is open to persons of any faith and affirms the role of spiritual faith in marriage without passing judgment on anyone's religious choices. Other denominationally specific Engaged Encounter programs are offered as well. (See "Resources for Marriage Enrichment Ministries" for contact information.)

Other Options

The Coalition for Marriage, Family, and Couples Education (CMFCE) provides extensive information about a variety of marriage education programs at their website (*www.smartmarriages.com*). Some of these programs are directed specifically toward engaged and newlywed couples. Others are suitable for couples at any state of relationship. You will find in the Resources section of this manual contact information for *Saving Your Marriage Before It Starts*, a complete curriculum kit. With so many resources available, pastors should not find it difficult to offer marriage education for engaged and newlywed couples in group settings.

Beyond the inherent values of offering group experiences for engaged and newlywed couples, your congregation is likely to experience additional benefits. Involving resource persons and married couples as leaders gives them an important way to serve in the ministry of their church. Leader couples will most likely find their own marriages enriched, thereby strengthening the institution of marriage within your church family. In addition, a supportive Christian community may develop for engaged and newly married couples and for the married couples who give leadership to these programs.

Invite members of your congregation to brainstorm with you how they can help educate couples for marriage and nurture them through their early years of adjustment. They may also want to consider support groups for couples facing various challenges: new parents; couples struggling with infertility; parents of teens; couples caring for elderly parents; or couples dealing with particular transitions or crises such as unemployment, illness, or a breakdown of their relationship. (See "Support for Couples in Transition and Crisis" in Chapter 10.)

10

COMPREHENSIVE
MARRIAGE MINISTRIES

"Do not be conformed to this world, but be transformed by the renewing of your minds, so that you may discern what is the will of God—what is good and acceptable and perfect" (Romans 12:2).

Would you like your church to be known as one that nurtures marriages and families? No one program or activity will earn that reputation for you. Many factors in congregational life, some subtle and others more obvious, weave together to create an environment that is "marriage-friendly" and "family-friendly"—or not. Church activities can pull family members in opposite directions, giving those who avoid intimacy yet another excuse for being too busy for those with whom they should be most closely connected. But churches can consciously affirm and support family relationships. A family-friendly environment need not exclude singles, but can minister to them by connecting them with families—their own or "adopted" ones, as well as through specialized programs to meet their particular needs.

Some suggestions for affirming and supporting marriages:

- Plan a Sweetheart Banquet for married couples on Valentine's Day.
- Make Mother's Day and Father's Day occasions for reflection on healthy relationships.
- Celebrate wedding anniversaries during worship.
- Recruit youth, young adults, and older adults to provide free child care for a couples' night out and for marriage enrichment events.

- Affirm those who decide to miss a church meeting in order to participate in a family event. There will always be another meeting!
- Encourage couples and families to work together on some projects.

Preaching and Teaching

In addition to such obvious gestures as those listed, a church's preaching and teaching can nurture attitudes that strengthen marriages and families. Sermons do not have to focus exclusively on marriage and family life for this purpose, but may simply incorporate themes and illustrations related to healthy relationships. Recently a pastor preaching on letting "the same mind be in you that was in Christ Jesus" (Philippians 2:5), pointed out that Jesus demonstrated personal concern for and interest in those who spoke to him. The preacher went on to comment that through marriage enrichment experiences, husbands and wives learn to really listen to each other. He used several anecdotes involving married couples, parents and children, and persons in other relationship contexts to illustrate how attentive listening communicates honor and respect. Examples from marriage and family life may be woven into many other topics, such as forgiveness, anger, conflict management, covenant, and faithful living.

Christian teaching calls us to discipleship and nurtures attitudes conducive to marital and family stability. People of faith are generally happier than other people, perhaps because they have a sense of belonging, a purpose in life, and a set of rules to guide their behavior. Religious convictions help people accept the ups and downs of human existence and assume responsibility for their decisions and actions. In contrast, the narcissistic belief that we are entitled to happiness, which seems to run rampant in our culture today, encourages persons to seek first their own satisfaction and to discard relationships that do not meet their expectations.[1] Christian teaching affirms that all persons are of sacred worth, that we are called to serve God in all aspects of our lives and in all of our relationships, and that dealing with disappointment and difficulties is a primary factor in spiritual growth.

Sometimes, however, organized religion endorses unhealthy and even dangerous attitudes and behaviors. Abused women who have been taught that God wants them to be submissive and that the husband is the head of the household, even when he is not submissive to God, may believe that their situation is God's will. If they feel that they are the cause of the husband's violence, they will hesitate to ask for help. The promise that our suffering on earth will be rewarded in heaven, while sometimes appropriate, can encourage persons to believe that they should put up with behaviors that are threatening to their safety and well-being. Pastors must communicate that Jesus' emphasis on forgiving others does not mean that one has to continue to be a victim. Scripture clearly communicates that God is a loving God and that right relationships are holy. A marriage covenant broken by violence may be restored through forgiveness, but the abuser must be required to "sin no more." In most cases, this will require professional intervention.[2]

Marriage and Family Ministries Team

A comprehensive marriage ministry requires the commitment and involvement of other church leaders besides the pastor. The Marriage and Family Ministries Team concept calls for establishing a team to develop and implement plans for supporting and nurturing marriages. Marriage and Family Ministries Teams involve the pastor and/or other church staff, volunteer lay couples, and professional consultants with training and expertise in related fields such as couple therapy, marriage enrichment, social services, or family medicine. Together this team assesses the needs in the congregation or parish and the available resources, developing whichever ministries they consider most important for their situation:

- marriage preparation;
- mentor couple programs;
- enrichment events for those already married;
- ministries to particular groups, such as new parents, couples caring for elderly parents, or couples in transition or crisis.[3]

Michael McManus offers training and resources for Marriage Savers Churches, which provide programs for and train mentors to work with couples who are seriously dating, engaged couples, married couples, those considering divorce, the separated, and those in blended families.[4] The type of mentoring varies according to those being served. Premarital mentoring (Chapter 8) involves one couple working with one couple, as does mentoring for troubled marriages. The best programs to strengthen existing marriages are group experiences (Chapter 9) in which couples learn skills, share stories, and provide mutual support. Blended families benefit most from regular meetings, perhaps biweekly, with support groups. Separated spouses are most effectively mentored by a friend of the same gender (See *Marriage 911: First Response and Manual to Create a Marriage Savers Congregation*, which details each of these ministries.)

Relationship Education for Children, Youth, and Young Adults

Churches can help persons develop the attitudes and behaviors needed to build lasting, fulfilling marriages, but we must recognize that we are working against a self-centered culture with high expectations for instant gratification. We have to convince our young people that some things are worth hard work and sacrifice. They need to hear the joyful witness of couples who delight in a stronger, richer relationship because they have hung in there through difficult times. In marriage, some days—some years—will be better than others. In the absence of abuse, there is much to be said for focusing on the positive and working through conflicts. Giving more than you receive and placing marriage and family above one's individual desires are values which, if nurtured early in life, might lead to fewer divorces and broken families, and to a more civil society.[5]

Our children and young people receive distorted messages about sexual behavior from the media and from contemporary culture. Society encourages us to treat sexual expression casually. Considering how frequently movies and television programs portray sexual intercourse as ordinary dating behavior or a recreational activity, it is not surprising to learn of increased sexual activity among preteens.[6] Some practice a "technical virginity," participating in mutual masturbation, oral sex, and other variations, but stopping short of actual penetration. Youth need to know that casual sexual encounters are exploitative and wrong and often disappointing. In such encounters each person treats his or her sexual desire as a physical drive isolated from any deeper psychological and emotional connection. Sexual intercourse as well as other sexual behaviors cannot be treated merely as a friendly gesture or as a response to sexual appetite and still retain the power to express devotion and commitment in covenantal relationships.[7] We need to teach young people that only faithful monogamy can assure the climate of trust necessary for passion to grow and deepen.[8]

Most denominations offer curriculum materials for children and youth that address relationship and sexuality issues. For children in preschool programs, The United Methodist Church offers *Wonder-filled Weekdays,* which helps children build positive relationships in the classroom and also explores family relationships. For school-age children in after-school programs, the *Bible Lessons for Youth* curriculum offers units focusing on building relationships. One unit, for example, provides lessons designed to help youth consider and make responsible decisions regarding sex, marriage, and singleness.

For older elementary students, The United Methodist Church provides *Created by God: Tweens, Faith, and Human Sexuality,* New Edition; and for teens, Teen Sexuality Resources. Both programs include a student booklet, a parent resource, and a leader's guide. *FaithMatters for Young Adults: Living the Faith* (Nashville: Abingdon Press, 2006)

addresses a variety of topics, including relationships, from a Christian perspective. Visit *www.cokesbury.com* or call 800-672-1789 for these and other curriculum resources.

In addition to denominational and ecumenical resources, some commercially packaged programs, such as *Connections,* designed for use in schools and youth organizations, can easily be supplemented with appropriate biblical and religious content and is scheduled for revision incorporating religious materials. This program is described in more detail with information about how to order in the Resources section. You might also check with your denominational office to see what is available there.

Many parenting resources provide spiritual support and practical advice on such issues as parent-child and parent-teen communication, step-parenting, discipline, teaching respect, managing anger, and resolving conflict. See the following web articles and their accompanying resource lists at *www.gbod.org/marriage*: "Empowering Parents" under the General Resources link and "Equipping Youth to Build Healthy Relationships" under the Relationship Education link.

Marriage Preparation Policy and Practices

Effective marriage preparation for couples who are seriously dating and for engaged couples may involve mentor couples (Chapter 8) and group experiences (Chapter 9) in addition to premarital counseling with the pastor (Chapters 4-7). A written statement can be prepared to explain the church's policy and practices in regard to weddings, expectations of those who use the church for weddings, and the various marriage preparation programs available. Such a document clarifies what will be required of couples and/or what options are available in terms of premarital counseling, mentoring, and group sessions, before and after the wedding. The worship committee or administrative council may also wish to establish guidelines for music, decorations, picture taking, videotaping, and the like in order to ensure the worshipful nature of the service.

One church's "Wedding Guidelines and Procedures" statement explains that the couple will be given daily Scripture passages to read on their own for the month before the wedding, invites them to participate in the worship life of the church, and encourages couples who are living together to find separate housing until after the wedding.[9] If you choose to encourage a premarital chastity covenant, as discussed in Chapter 3 you can use a statement like that in *A Manual to Create a Marriage Savers Congregation* or design one of your own.

Other points that could be addressed in a "Wedding Guidelines and Procedures" statement include the following:

1. Commentary on the meaning of Christian marriage
2. Statement regarding who may be married in this church
   A. Members
   B. Nonmembers at the discretion of the pastor
   C. Divorced persons at the discretion of the pastor
3. Limitations
   A. Pastor's approval for all weddings to be performed in the church
   B. Pastor to invite any other minister whose participation is desired
   C. Saturday evenings, Christmas Eve, and Holy Week to be considered only under special circumstances
   D. Weddings scheduled far enough in advance to allow for adequate preparation
4. Requirements and/or recommendations for marriage preparation
   A. Minimum number of premarital counseling sessions with the pastor
   B. Use of workbook, study guide, or other materials
   C. Participation in mentor couples program and/or group activities
   D. Participation in the worship life of the church
   E. Engagement Ceremony (Appendix I)
5. Expectations regarding the wedding ceremony
   A. Christian liturgy; denominational resource usually used
   B. Openness to couple's creativity and input within limits
6. Support services
   A. Consultation with organist and pastor regarding musical selections
   B. Use of church facilities for dressing before the ceremony

   C. Provision of a printed bulletin or program through the church office at minimal cost
7. Recommendations in regard to decorations
   A. Types of candelabra and other items available at the church
   B. Items that may be rented through a florist
   C. Requirement for drip-less candles
   D. Limitations on use of tape or thumbtacks
8. Photography and videotaping
   A. Limitations on flash photography during the ceremony
   B. Suggestion that formal photographs be taken before the ceremony as a courtesy to guests
   C. Videotaping only from a stationary and discrete position
9. Wedding receptions at the church
   A. Space couples may reserve, maximum seating capacity
   B. Arrangements with a church group or outside caterer
   C. Prohibitions against use of alcohol and tobacco
   D. Request for use of birdseed instead of rice or confetti, and appropriate location for such "greeting"
10. Fees and honorariums
    A. Church facilities available to members at no cost, although an additional gift may be made at the couple's discretion
    B. Charges for nonmembers to use the sanctuary and fellowship hall, including custodial fees
    C. Expectations in regard to honorariums for the pastor and/or organist and/or other church staff

Visit *www.gbod.org/marriage* and select the link Marriage Preparation for "Best Practices in Marriage Preparation," "Premarital Inventories," and other articles and resource reviews.

Enrichment Opportunities for Married Couples

A study conducted by the Catholic Church in 1995 found that while most couples who had participated in a marriage preparation program rated it as a valuable experience, couples in the early years of their marriage valued it most. Since couples who had been married longer tended to value the marriage preparation program less, it is apparently not realistic to expect that experience to prepare a couple adequately for a lifetime.[10] If we understand "becoming married" as a process that takes place over time rather than a one-time event, we will incorporate in-marriage education as an integral part of our ministries.[11]

In *Close Companions*, David Mace points out that engaged couples are often incapable of appreciating and integrating information provided in premarital sessions, simply because they do not yet have the experience of being married. Counseling is available when the couple, or one of the partners, becomes desperate enough to ask for help, but assistance could be offered during the critical early years in order to prevent serious relationship breakdowns. During the first months of marriage, behavior patterns are more fluid and open to influence. By the end of the first year of marriage, relationship patterns are more firmly ingrained, and the best opportunity for helping couples fine-tune their relationship may have passed. Mace notes that the "intermarital taboo" keeps couples isolated, thinking they are the only ones struggling with adjustments and crises.[12] By emphasizing the importance of growth experiences and marriage education for newlyweds and throughout the marital life cycle, churches can change the norm. We wish that more persons would share the insight of a young wife who declared, "I just assumed that if you want a strong marriage, you get involved in a support group."

Marriage enrichment experiences, whether weekend retreats or special evening programs or ongoing support groups, provide opportunities for couples to restore and nurture the positive aspects of their relationship. Most such events invite couples to affirm each other, recall happy times they have shared, and make plans for activities they enjoy doing together. At the same time, couples . learn that conflict is a normal part of intimate relationships and that certain attitudes and behaviors can help them work through their differences without damaging their relationship. There is real value in bringing together multi-generational groups of couples. Youthful energy and idealism stimulate older couples to recall and rejoice in their journeys thus far, while the wisdom and perspective of the elders encourages the confidence of the young that they can make it through whatever challenges they face.

Another approach would be to offer "booster" courses, support groups, and/or mentoring for cou-

ples at key learning moments, such as when the first child is born, when children become teenagers, or when children leave home. Other special needs or issues around which groups could be formed include unemployment, two-career marriages, dealing with serious illness, and caring for elderly parents. In addition to Alcoholics Anonymous and AlAnon groups, couples dealing with addictions might benefit from couple support groups designed to meet their particular needs.

In the Resources section you will find information about support groups and several different marriage enrichment programs. Some of these, such as Better Marriages (formerly The Association for Couples in Marriage Enrichment) and Marriage Encounter, require specific training. Others can be led by anyone with basic group leadership skills and some understanding of marriage issues. A variety of other marriage education courses are listed on the Coalition for Marriage, Family and Couples Education website, *www.smartmarriages.com*, and in the resource documents at *www.marriagelovepower.net* and *www. gbod.org/marriage*.

Support for Couples in Special Situations, Transitions, and Crisis

Couples seeking help typically wait six years from the time storm clouds surface in their marriage before asking for any kind of professional advice. By then it is often too late.[13] Even more likely, they do not seek help at all. Often when a divorce is announced in a congregation, it comes as a complete surprise to people who thought they knew the couple well. On the other hand, church leaders, even when aware of a couple's difficulties, often do not know how to help. One woman reports:

When my ex-husband and I were going through marriage difficulties that resulted in a separation and divorce, we were still active in our church. My ex-husband was a ruling elder and I was the Sunday school superintendent. He and I served as the youth group advisors and also participated in couple's gatherings sponsored by the church. Yet when we began to tell others within the church about our relationship breakdown, and even during our separation, not one of the clergy or lay leaders of the church ever offered to assist us or to help us find someone who could counsel with us. My faith community was silent during one of the most crucial times in my life. I was angry, not at God, but at the church. The six months following our separation was the only time in my adult life (I was 27 at the time) that I was not an active participant in a faith community.

Perhaps the church leadership in this situation were just not equipped to minister to a couple in crisis, but there is no excuse today for such neglect. A wealth of new resources and programs, some of which are described in the Resources section of this manual, offer hope and practical assistance for couples in troubled relationships, Michele Weiner-Davis and Susan Page, among others, have written books detailing how one person can change the dynamics of a relationship, even when the other refuses to participate in counseling or in a relationship-healing program. By taking responsibility for one's own attitudes and behaviors and learning to be less reactive, an individual can break through negative cycles and begin the process of building a more positive relationship. Support groups for wives and/or husbands who want to try such an approach could make a substantial difference for families in conflict. You might find *Before You Divorce*, described in the Resources section, a useful tool for motivating couples not to give up too easily on their relationship.

Before referring couples for therapy, you need to locate counselors who have appropriate training and commitment to rebuilding relationships. Couples considering marital counseling may need encouragement and assistance in assessing a potential therapist's background, training, attitudes, and approach. They should avoid therapists who cannot document significant education and experience in working with couples or those who express more interest in helping individuals than in salvaging troubled marriages.[14] Look instead for those who offer skills training or at least encourage participation in marriage education programs.[15]

Some churches now offer mentoring ministries for couples in crisis. Father Dick McGinnis, in Jacksonville, Florida, announced from the pulpit that he wanted to meet with couples whose marriages had been in trouble but who had recovered and reconciled. Ten couples showed up for that meeting, and seven of them agreed to join him in sharing how they had been healed. From that process they developed Marriage Ministry action steps similar in concept to the Twelve Steps for Alcoholics Anonymous and began a ministry to hurting couples.[16] We know of other churches where a similar process is now underway because couples who have weathered a stormy period in their marriage want to help others experience the same grace and joy. Several organizations such as A New Beginning, The Beyond Affairs Network and The Third Option (See Resources) now offer programs for couples in crisis. *Marriage 911: First Response* helps couples find healing by focusing on their relationship with God. A workbook designed for use with a same-sex support partner helps an individual deal with his or her own issues, regardless of what his or her spouse decides to do.

Another significant marriage-healing ministry is Retrouvaille, "a Christian Peer Ministry and a Lifeline for Troubled Marriages." Beginning with a weekend retreat in which husbands and wives are helped to reestablish communication and gain new understanding of themselves and each other, the program also includes follow-up sessions over a three-month period. Presenting couples, who have experienced their own crises, share stories of pain, reconciliation, and healing. Participants are not asked to share publicly in this setting, but learn tools and receive encouragement to rediscover each other and their relationship.[17] Couples who have experienced healing through Retrouvaille would be a wonderful resource for mentoring other couples in crisis. Contact information is provided in the Resources section.

You will, of course, still need to minister to divorcing and divorced couples and help them learn from their experiences. Persons need to understand their own contribution to a relationship's breakdown before they marry again, lest they repeat their mistakes. Remarriage is much more complicated than most couples expect, especially if there are children involved. See the Resources section in this manual for resources related to divorce recovery, remarriage, and blending families. Visit *www.marriagelove-power.net*, *www.gbod.org/marriage*, and *www.gbod.org/family* for more recommended resources.

Finally, pastors must learn more about domestic violence and how to minister effectively to those caught up in that dynamic. Pastors untrained in this area often discount the danger. Offering simplistic and spiritualized solutions to this very complicated problem can be a tragic mistake. The usual strategies for healing troubled relationships do not apply, and priority must be given to the safety of the victim. Do not attempt to bring such a couple together for counseling, but do provide emotional and practical support for the victim and hold the abuser accountable for getting into treatment.[18]

Community Marriage Agreements

Michael McManus campaigns vigorously for churches to join with other churches in their communities to establish common guidelines for marriage and family ministries. Although such agreements initially addressed marriage preparation only, most now include programs to strengthen existing marriages and save troubled ones. Typical guidelines for marriage preparation include requirements for:

- at least four months of marriage preparation;
- use of a premarital inventory;
- meeting with a mentor couple to discuss issues on the inventory;
- participation in marriage education or engagement seminars.

In a typical community recently, pastors also pledged to:

- require at least two postmarital counseling sessions with a mentor couple, six months after the wedding and again at one year;
- encourage all married couples to attend a marriage enrichment retreat;
- create a mentoring ministry in which couples whose marriages once nearly failed help couples who are experiencing troubled relationships;
- cooperate in learning more about how to help couples bond for life;
- participate in programs to strengthen their own marriages.

McManus reports significant drops in the divorce rate in those cities where clergy have joined in such commitments.[19] He also reports the establishment of successful programs for reconciling separated couples and supporting blended families. A sample policy and a detailed outline of "Ten Steps to Create a Community Marriage Policy®" may be obtained from Marriage Savers,® Inc. (See contact information in the Resources section.)

Influencing Public Policy

The authors of *From Culture Wars to Common Ground: Religion and the American Family Debate* challenge churches not only to help their members and constituents form and sustain strong families, but also to participate in shaping public policy and restoring a positive marriage culture in society. What is happening in the larger community affects us all, and we cannot isolate ourselves by thinking we are responsible only for "our own." Some marriage supporters direct their energies toward making the workplace more family-friendly, providing more adequate supports for parents, and challenging the media "to tell better stories about human love, sexuality, marriage, and families." Others push for legislation mandating marriage education, strengthening marriage preparation, and requiring counseling before and during divorce proceedings.[20] See the Coalition for Marriage, Family, and Couples Education, LLC website for updated information on legislative and other marriage-strengthening initiatives. See also *www.childwelfare.gov* for concrete marriage-strengthening suggestions for parents, families, faith communities, civic leaders, the legal profession, youth workers, marriage counselors, educators, medical professionals, and government agencies.

In addition to helping shape public policy, churches can offer practical assistance to the community at large by encouraging and supporting marriage education in the public sector in cooperation with schools, colleges, employee assistance programs, and social service agencies. Although welfare reform in the 1990's authorized states to use Temporary Aid to Needy Families (TANF) funds to promote forming and maintaining two-parent families, no states undertook such initiatives at first. In March 2000, however, Governor Keating of Oklahoma announced his intention to use $10,000,000 of federal block grant funds "to encourage healthy, stable marriages as a way of reducing divorce, out-of-wedlock child-bearing, and welfare dependency." Although some critics have questioned whether government ought to be promoting marriage, Wade Horn, president of the National Fatherhood Initiative, points to evidence that communities with high marriage rates have less crime and less welfare dependency than those with lower marriage rates. He declares, "If marriage is good for communities, why should government be shy about promoting and strengthening it?"[21]

A more positive attitude toward marriage in our society at large, along with increased public awareness of effective family-strengthening strategies, would make it easier for pastors to involve engaged couples in effective marriage preparation programs. It seems likely that churches working toward restoring a pro-marriage culture would attract positive publicity and new members as well. An even more important motivation for the church to exert its influence in the public sector, however, is its call to serve as the yeast which "leavens the whole batch of dough." (1 Corinthians 5:6). Society desperately needs the people of God to take on the mission of strengthening marriages and restoring families to wholeness and health.

Appendix 1

ENGAGEMENT CEREMONY*

For Use in Congregational Worship or Other Settings

Liturgist: With great joy we announce to this congregation the engagement of _____ and _____. They come before you today to declare their intention to prepare earnestly for their life together and to seek your blessing and support. Genesis 2:24 states God's plan for a man and a woman to leave their respective families and form a new unit. The apostle Paul, in his letter to the church at Ephesus, instructs them to "be subject to one another out of reverence for Christ." _____ and _____, is it your intention to build a marriage relationship based on faith and on the Christian principles of unselfish love, forgiveness, and grace?

Engaged Couple: Yes, that is our intention and our desire. Will the church surround us with prayer and support us in our preparation for marriage so that we may truly discern God's will for us and grow in our knowledge and understanding of ourselves and each other?

Congregation: With God's help, we will.

Engaged Couple: Will you continue to grow in your own relationships, modeling for us the kind of love that "bears all things, believes all things, hopes all things, endures all things"? (1 Corinthians 13:7).

Congregation: With God's help, we will.

Liturgist: _____ and _____ have committed to participate in [as applicable—premarital counseling, our mentoring program, group sessions, personal study, and prayer], that their marriage relationship may benefit from the wisdom and training of others and that they may be blessed and strengthened to serve God faithfully in their life together. Let us pray. Creator God, we thank you for the love that has brought _____ and _____ together and for the commitment they make today to prepare for a marriage that honors you and conforms to your will. May their life together serve as a sign and an instrument of Christ's love in a hurting world. Grant us wisdom and will to guide them through this time of preparation, with gratitude for all that you have given to us along life's way; in Christ's name we pray. Amen.

*This liturgy is based on suggestions and discussions regarding engagement ceremonies shared in the Religion, Culture, and Family Project on-line newsletter, June 2 and July 14, 2000 (*www.uchicago.edu/divinity/family/backissueslengagement.html*).

Appendix II
MENTORING COVENANT*

- We believe that man and woman are created in God's image and that God loves us and wants us to grow in love, mutual satisfaction, and joy.
- We believe that God established the sanctity and companionship of marriage and that God calls us to stay together for life.
- We believe that we are accountable to God and to each other for the quality of our marriage.
- We believe that every couple can continue to grow in love through every stage in life.
- We believe that a mentor couple and a partner couple can learn from each other through open, honest communication.

The Partner Couple agrees to:
- Pray for God's guidance and direction in our marriage preparation and seek God's blessing for our marriage.
- Attend worship together as often as possible.
- Participate faithfully in couple and group sessions with our mentor couple and be open to learning from them.
- Share openly and honestly with our mentor couple.
- Honor confidentiality in regard to personal experiences that the mentor couple may share.
- Meet with the pastor to plan the wedding ceremony and to seek additional guidance as needed.

The Mentor Couple agrees to:
- Pray for and with the partner couple, seeking God's guidance and blessing for their marriage.
- Attend worship together as often as possible.
- Honestly examine and strive to strengthen and enrich our own marriage.
- Listen to the needs and concerns of the partner couple while facilitating their discussions.
- Honor the confidentiality of all discussions, the only exception being when we need to seek additional guidance from the pastor.
- Participate in monthly meetings for nurture, education, supervision, and support for ourselves and for other mentor couples.

Partner Couple:
_____

Pastor:
_____

Mentor Couple:
_____

Date:
_____

* Developed by the Caring Couples Ministry of Forrest Burdette United Methodist Church, Hurricane, West Virginia.

Appendix III

MENTOR COUPLE PARTICIPATION IN WEDDING CEREMONY*

The following liturgy may be inserted at an appropriate place in the wedding ceremony, perhaps following the Greeting or just before the Exchange of Vows. The mentor couple husband and wife may divide up their parts as they wish.

Liturgist: Our church initiated a ministry we call Caring Couples [or other]. Part of this ministry involves matching an engaged couple with a mentor couple who shares personally with them and guides them through the marriage preparation process. _____ and _____ have served as mentors to _____ and _____, using the GROWING LOVE IN CHRISTIAN MARRIAGE premarital inventory and Couple's Manual [or other].

Mentor Couple: We have been meeting with _____ and _____ since _____, as they have prepared not just for this wedding day, but for a lifetime together. They have been learning communication and problem-solving skills and setting goals for growth in their relationship. They have seen that marriage requires consistent effort and provides opportunities for mutual support within a loving, God-ordained relationship. Now we present to them the Marriage Covenant they have signed, which reads:

[Marriage Covenant, from GROWING LOVE IN CHRISTIAN MARRIAGE Couple's Manual or other resource, may be read by the couple to be wed or by the mentor couple.]

Mentor Couple: _____ and _____, we have been blessed through this time of sharing with you and we promise, along with your family and friends gathered here today, to continue to prayerfully support and encourage you in these vows you are about to make. May God abundantly bless you always.

* This liturgy is based on a ritual developed by the Caring Couples Ministry of Forrest Burdette United Methodist Church in Hurricane, West Virginia. The Marriage Covenant is framed and then placed on the altar after it is read during the wedding ceremony.

Appendix IV

PLANNING GUIDE/ CHECKLIST

Guide/Checklist for Establishing
Comprehensive Marriage Preparation Ministries

Mark each item with a dot when you begin work on it; after you complete that task, change the dot to a check and indicate the date. Write NA if the item is not applicable. The numbers in parentheses indicate which pages in this manual provide information relevant to that item. Steps do not necessarily have to be completed in sequential order.

Recruit a team to plan and coordinate marriage and family ministries (Chapter 10)   _____

Increase knowledge about the pastor's role in marriage preparation Chapters 1, 3-7)   _____

Increase knowledge about marriage and family ministries (Chapters 2 and 10)   _____

Increase knowledge about other strategies for marriage preparation (Chapters 8, 9)   _____

Research programs and resources available   _____

    Check with nearby counseling centers and other pastors   _____

    Contact national offices of programs that interest you (Resources)   _____

    List here courses or programs in which you can participate

    List here books you want to read

Explore cooperative projects, such as a community marriage agreement (Chapter 10)   _____

Outline your basic approach for premarital counseling (Appendix V)   _____

Create a comfortable setting for your premarital counseling (Chapter 1)   _____

Establish a consultative relationship with a therapist or counselor (Chapter 1)   _____

Establish a record-keeping system for your premarital counseling (Chapter 4)   _____

Develop a church policy statement for weddings/marriage preparation (Chapter 10)   _____

Organize a mentor couples program (Chapter 8)   _____

Plan group sessions for engaged and/or newlywed couples (Chapter 9)   _____

Establish a plan for post-wedding contacts with couples (Chapter 7)   _____

Integrate relationship education into programs for children, youth,
and young adults (Chapter 10 and the Resources section)   _____

Establish marriage education and enrichment programs (Chapter 10 and
the Resources section)   _____

Establish ministries for couples with special needs (Chapter 10)   _____

Establish ministries for couples in crisis (Chapter 10 and the Resources section)   _____

Develop strategies for influencing public opinion and policy (Chapter 10)   _____

Appendix V

GUIDE/CHECKLIST FOR MARRIAGE PREPARATION WITH COUPLES

(Duplicate for Use With Each Couple)

Mark each item with a dot when you begin work on it; after you complete that task, change the dot to a check and indicate the date. Write NA if the item is not applicable, MC if a Mentor Couple will do it, and GR if this will be dealt with in a group setting. Steps do not necessarily have to be completed in sequential order.

Name or Code for Couple _____

Schedule first session with couple   _____

Share expectations for marriage preparation   _____

Give couple statement of church policy   _____

Schedule engagement ceremony   _____

Share information about mentor couples   _____

Share information about group events for engaged couples   _____

Give couple copies of the GROWING LOVE IN CHRISTIAN MARRIAGE Couple's Manual   _____

Give or recommend other reading material   _____

Receive and review the couple's Wedding Information form   _____

Read through marriage ritual with the couple   _____

Discuss modifications to the service   _____

Discuss their previous marriage preparation   _____

Discuss faith issues   _____

Administer Marriage Lifestyle Questionnaire   _____

Introduce the Growing Love in Christian Marriage Couple's Manual   _____

Explain premarital sexual covenant   _____

Schedule individual appointments   _____

Schedule next couple session(s)   _____

Discuss Marriage Lifestyle Questionnaire responses with individuals   _____

Review Marriage Lifestyle Questionnaire responses with couple   _____

Schedule other individual appointments if needed   _____

Evaluate the couple's progress with them   _____

Make referral for any specific concerns   _____

Inquire about their experience with mentor couple   _____

Discuss their use of the Couple's Manual   _____

Inquire about their experience in group session(s)   _____

Finalize plans for the wedding service   _____

Finalize plans for the rehearsal   _____

Receive their wedding license   _____

Work on specific issues raised by the couple or individuals. List issues here.   _____

Work on developmental tasks:

   developing a faith-based lifestyle   _____

   developing effective communication   _____

   providing for necessities   _____

   managing finances   _____

   establishing roles   _____

   meeting personal needs   _____

   planning for children   _____

adjusting to relatives   _____

making and keeping friends   _____

taking part in community life   _____

Summarize learnings and plan for future growth-nurturing activities   _____

Invite couple to participate in postwedding group activities   _____

Invite couple to meet with you again after the wedding   _____

Evaluation form delivered to couple   _____

Date requested for return   _____

Evaluation form completed and returned   _____

Follow-up suggested by evaluation responses. (List below and check when completed.)

Notes

Introduction

1. Linda J. Waite, "Does Marriage Matter?" *Demography*, Vol. 32, No. 4, (November 1995), pp. 483-507.
2. David Popenoe and Barbara Dafoe Whitehead, *The Slate of Our Unions: The Social Health of Marriage in America*, 1999 (New Brunswick, NJ: The National Marriage Project. Rutgers University, June 1999), p. 3.
3. Paul R. Amato and Alan Booth, *A Generation at Risk: Growing Up In an Era of Family Upheaval* (Cambridge, MA: Harvard University Press, 1997), pp. 219-21.
   Michael J. McManus, *Marriage Savers®: Helping Your Friends and Family Avoid Divorce* (Grand Rapids, MI: Zondervan, 1995), pp. 29-48.
4. Judith S. Wallerstein and Sandra Blakeslee, *Second Chances: Men, Women, and Children a Decade After Divorce* (New York: Ticknor and Fields, 1989), p. xii.
5. McManus, op. cit., pp. 20, 24.
6. David Arp and Claudia Arp, *The Second Half of Marriage* (Grand Rapids, MI: Zondervan, 1996), p. 36.
   John Gottman, with Nan Silver, *Why Marriages Succeed or Fail* (New York: Simon & Schuster, 1994), p. 28.
7. David Olsen, quoted by Michael J. McManus in *Marriage Savers®*, p. 113.

Chapter 1

1. Herbert Anderson, "Marital Preparation—A Protestant Perspective," *The Family Handbook*, eds. Herbert Anderson, Don Browning, Ian S. Evison, and Mary Stewart Van Leeuwen (Louisville, KY: Westminster John Knox, 1998), p. 117.
2. McManus, *Marriage Savers®*, p. 295.
3. *The Book of Discipline of The United Methodist Church, 2012* (Nashville, TN: The United Methodist Publishing House,), ¶ 340 (.3a).
4. Warren and Mary Ebinger, *Do-lt-Yourself Marriage Enrichment: A Workshop on Your Own Time, on Your Own Terms, on Your Own Turf* (Nashville, TN: Abingdon Press, 1998), pp. 17-18.

Chapter 2

1. *The Book of Discipline of The United Methodist Church, 2012* (Nashville. TN: The United Methodist Publishing House), ¶ 161 (f).
2. "A Service of Christian Marriage," *The United Methodist Hymnal* (Nashville, TN: The United Methodist Publishing House, 2000), p. 865.
3. Ibid., p. 867.
4. Willard F. Harley, Jr., *His Needs, Her Needs: Building An Affair-Proof Marriage* (Grand Rapids, MI: Fleming H. Revell, 1994), pp. 19-20.
5. Harville Hendrix, *Getting the Love You Want* (New York: Harper & Row, 1988), pp. 33-40.

Chapter 3

1. David Augsburger, *Sustaining Love: Healing and Growth in the Passages of Marriage* (Ventura, CA: Regal, 1988), pp. 12-14.
2. Robert A. Johnson, *We: Understanding the Psychology of Romantic Love* (San Francisco: Harper & Row, 1983), p. 193.
3. Robert A. Johnson, *She: Understanding Feminine Psychology* (King of Prussia, PA: Religious Publishing, 1976), p. 39.
4. Deborah Tannen, *You Just Don't Understand: Women and Men in Conversation* (New York, Ballentine Books, 1990), pp. 18, 294.
5. John Gray, *What Your Mother Couldn't Tell You and Your Father Didn't Know: Advanced Relationship Skills for Better Communication and Lasting Intimacy* (New York: HarperCollins, 1994), pp. 87-88.
6. Robert Johnson, *He: Understanding Masculine Psychology* (King of Prussia, PA: Religious Publishing, 1974), pp. 3-5.
7. William J. Doherty, quoted in *From Culture Wars to Common Ground: Religion and the American Family Debate* by Don S. Browning, Bonnie J. Miller-McLemore, Pamela D. Couture, K. Brynolf Lyon, and Robert M. Franklin (Louisville, KY: Westminster John Knox, 1997), p. 319.
8. *Ministry to Interchurch Marriages: A National Study* (Omaha, NE: Center for Marriage and Family, Creighton University, 1999), pp. 7-8.
9. Ibid., p. 140.
10. David R. Mace, *Close Companions: The Marriage Enrichment Handbook* (New York: Continuum, 1982), p. 113.
11. Catherine M. Wallace, *For Fidelity: How Intimacy and Commitment Enrich Our Lives* (New York: Alfred A. Knopf, 1998), p. 59.
12. Harriet McManus, "A Case for Abstinence," *The Marriage Saver I*, Vol. 6 (Potomac, MD: Marriage Savers, February/March 2000), p. 7.

13. Ibid., p. 7.
14. Michael J. McManus, *A Manual On How to Create a Marriage Savers® Congregation* (Bethesda, MD: Marriage Savers, 1999), p. 84.
15. David Popenoe and Barbara Dafoe Whitehead, *The State of Our Unions*, p. 11.
16. David and Vera Mace, *How to Have a Happy Marriage: A Step-by-Step Guide to an Enriched Relationship* (Nashville, TN: Abingdon Press, 1977), pp. 106-07.
17. David Mace, *Close Companions*, p. 192.

Chapter 4

1. Michael J. McManus, *A Manual on How to Create a Marriage Savers® Congregation*, p. 87.
2. Herbert Anderson, *The Family Handbook*, p. 115.
3. Scott Stanley, *Coalition for Marriage, Family, and Couples Education*, LLC (CMFCE), e-mail list service, August 18, 1999, page 2. Available at the CMFCE website (*www.smartmarriages.com*) under "Archives."
4. Don Browning, et. al., *From Culture Wars to Common Ground*, p. 309.
5. Everett L. Worthington, Jr., *Marriage Counseling: A Christian Approach to Counseling Couples* (Downers Grove, IL: InterVarsity Press, 1989), pp. 111-15.

Chapter 6

1. William C. Nichols, *Marital Therapy: An Integrative Approach* (New York: Guilford Press, 1988), pp. 20, 21, 26.
2. Evelyn Millis Duvall, *Marriage and Family Development* (Philadelphia: J.B. Lippincott, 1977), pp. 176-77.
3. *The United Methodist Hymnal* (Nashville, TN: The United Methodist Publishing House, 1989), p. 868.

Chapter 7

1. T*he Book of Discipline of The United Methodist Church, 2012* (Nashville: The United Methodist Publishing House), ¶ 162(k); ¶ 162 (v).
2. Edwin H. Friedman, *Generation to Generation: Family Process in Church and Synagogue* (New York: Guilford Press, 1985), pp. 13, 31.

Chapter 8

1. Dennis Lowe, Emily Scott-Lowe, and Sara Jackson, "Marriage Mentors: Experienced Guides Who Help Couples Navigate the Journey of Marriage" [paper presented at Coalition for Marriage, Family, and Couples Education, July 11, 1998] Malibu, CA: Center for the Family at Pepperdine University, 1998), pp. 2-5.
2. Sherod Miller, Phyllis Miller, Elam W. Nunnally, Daniel B. Wackman, *Talking and Listening Together: Couple Communication I* (Littleton, CO: Interpersonal Communication Programs, 1991), pp. 52-63.

Chapter 9

1. Richard Hunt and Joan Hunt, *Caring Couples Network Handbook* (Nashville, TN: Discipleship Resources, 1996), pp. 51-53.

Chapter 10

1. Frank Pittman, *Grow Up! How Taking Responsibility Can Make You a Happy Adult* (New York: Golden Books, 1998), pp. 18, 34, 39.
2. Marie M. Fortune, *Keeping the Faith: Questions and Answers for the Abused Woman* (San Francisco: Harper & Row, 1987), pp. 15-17, 35, 46, 47, 50,51,81-85.
3. Richard and Joan Hunt, *Caring Couples Network Handbook*, pp. 26, 27, 30, 31.
4. Michael J. McManus, *A Manual on How to Create a Marriage Savers® Congregation*, p. 24.
5. Kathleen Parker, *Happy Marriage—Oxymoron*. Syndicated column, July 15, 1999, p. 2. Available at the CMFCE website (*www.smartmarriages. com*) under "Archives."
6. Anne Jarrell, "Puppy Lust: The Face of Sex Grows Younger and Younger," *Sunday Gazette-Mail* (Charleston, WV, April 16, 2000), pp. 1C, 6C.
7. Catherine Wallace, *For Fidelity*, pp. 58-60, 69.
8. John Gray, *What Your Mother Couldn't Tell You*, pp. 4, 406.
9. First United Methodist Church Wedding Guidelines and Procedures (Buckhannon, WV: First United Methodist Church, 1997), pp. 1-5.
10. *Marriage Preparation in the Catholic Church: Getting It Right* (Omaha, NE; Center for Mamage and Family, Creighton University, 1995) p. 3.
11. Herbert Anderson, "Marriage Preparation," *The Family Handbook*, p. 117.
12. David Mace, *Close Companions*, pp. 196-98.
13. Diane Sollee, "Shifting Gears: An Optimistic View of the Future of Marriage" (paper presented at the Conference on Communitarian ProFamily Policies, Washington, DC, November 15,1996), p. 5. Available at the CMFCE website (*www.smartmarriages.com*) under "Articles."
14. William J. Doherty, "How Therapy Can Be Hazardous to Your Marital Health" (presented at the Coalition for Marriage, Family, and Couples Education (CMFCE) Conference, Washington, DC, July 3, 1999), pp. 8, 9. Available at the CMFCE website (*www.smartmarriages.com*) under "Articles."
15. Diane Sollee, "Shifting Gears," p. 11.
16. Michael McManus, *Marriage Savers®*, pp. 201-11.
17. *Is Your Marriage Tearing You Apart?* Brochure for Retrouvaille: A Christian Peer Ministry and Lifeline for Troubled Marriages. Call (800) 470-2230 for literature and information.
18. Al Miles, *Domestic Violence: What Every Pastor Needs to Know* (Minneapolis, MN: Fortress, 1000), pp. 122-26, 147-51, 181.
19. Michael McManus, *A Manual on How to Create a Marriage Savers® Congregation*, p. 19.

20. Don S. Browning, Bonnie J. Miller-McLemore, Pamela D. Couture, K. Brynolf Lyon, and Robert M. Franklin, *From Culture Wars to Common Ground: Religion and the American Family Debate* (Louisville, KY: Westminster John Knox, 1997), pp. 322-333.

21. Wade Horn, "Use Welfare Money to Promote Marriage" (Coalition for Marriage, Family and Couples Education, LLC (CMFCE) list service, April 4, 2000), pp. 2-3. Available at the CMFCE website (*www.smartmarriages.com*) under "Archives."

RESOURCES

Resources for Marriage and Family Ministries

Churches looking to strengthen their marriage and family ministries can choose from a variety of resources to supplement what is presented in this manual, thanks to extensive research and program development in this field. In addition to books, curriculum kits, and DVDs, websites and Facebook links now provide easy access to information and help. Most of the materials and resources listed and described in this section are written from a Christian perspective. Others, although written in secular language, are clearly compatible with Christian teaching (as summarized in Chapter 2 of this Manual) and can be easily adapted for church use by adding Scripture and worship resources. Secular resources, in fact, might be more appropriate for community outreach or for those less comfortable with religious language. You will find new books and resources in the following list, as well as some older "classics" that are still available, and some offered in other than English language versions. Many of the books sold by popular booksellers are also available as electronic downloads.

The expanded version of this resource list found online at *www.marriagelovepower.com* and the annotated lists and reviews posted at *www.gbod. org/marriage* and *www.gbod.org/family* describe even more resources; and in some cases, provide more detailed descriptions, which we hope you will find educational and informative. We will update these online lists from time to time to include new resources and to keep contact information and website addresses current. At these websites you will also find a schedule of upcoming training events and a directory of United Methodists trained in various programs and available for consultation and/or leadership. Visit websites for specific programs to find workshop schedules and locations and links for finding trained leaders. Cooperative parishes could collaborate in bringing leadership to an area or in purchasing resource materials to strengthen their marriage and family ministries.

Resources for Comprehensive Marriage
and Family Ministries   pages 91-92

Resources for Relationship Education
for Children, Youth, and Young Adults
pages 92-95

Resources for Marriage Preparation Ministries
pages 95-98

Resources for Marriage Education
and Enrichment Ministries
pages 98-103

Resources for Ministries With Families
in Special Situations, Transition, and Crisis
pages 103-106

Resources for Comprehensive Marriage and Family Ministries

Reading List for Comprehensive Marriage and Family Ministries

Blessed Be the Bond: Christian Perspectives on Marriage and Family, by William Johnson Everett (Lanham, Maryland: University Press of America, Inc., 1990). Although this book is now out of print, in 2011 the author made a free revised and updated version available as a download at *www.WilliamEverett.com/books-and-articles-free/*. The author explores social changes that have taken place in the way we think about marriage and family life, emphasizing the theological concepts of sacrament, covenant, vocation, communion, and marriage as a "manifestation of God's redemptive purposes in re-creating our world."

"Cultivating Compassionate Connection," by Jane P. Ives, *www.gbod.org/marriage*. Web article formatted for download and distribution.

Family Ministries Desk Reference: Holistic Responses to Contemporary Challenges, by Patricia D. Fosarelli (Louisville: Westminster John Knox Press, 2003). The author addresses a number of common challenges experienced by families (addition of new members, loss, single parenting, blending families, caring for aging parents, parenting adolescents, moving, substance abuse, depression). After clarifying physical and emotional aspects of these challenges, the author proposes specific individual and congregational responses and relevant resources for effective ministries in each situation.

Nonviolent Communication: A Language of Life, by Marshall B. Rosenberg, Ph.D. (Encinitas, CA: PuddleDancer Press, 2003), *www.nonviolentcommunication.com*. This clear and straightforward text shows how to break patterns of thinking that lead to arguments and anger and how to communicate with mutual respect and understanding. Separating observation from evaluation, taking responsibility for our feelings, making requests instead of demands, and listening empathically can enhance any relationship. This book works well with groups of individuals whether they are part of a couple or not. At the website, you will find a Companion Workbook excellent for group study and a variety of related books for parents, teachers, community leaders, etc. See also the review of this organization on page 92.

"Marriage and Family Ministry Starts in Our Homes," by Jane P. Ives, *www.gbod.org/marriage*. Web article formatted for download and distribution.

"Nurturing Families, Nurturing Disciples," by Jane P. Ives, *www.gbod.org/marriage*. Web article formatted for download and distribution.

"United Methodist Marriage and Family Ministries: Not for Couples Only," by Jane P. Ives, *www.gbod.org/marriage*. Web article formatted for download and distribution.

Program Resources for Comprehensive Marriage and Family Ministries

A Manual to Create a Marriage Savers Congregation, by Michael J. McManus (Potomac, Maryland: Marriage Savers, Inc., 1999), 9311 Harrington Drive, Potomac, MD 20854, 301-469-5873, *harriet@marriagesavers.org*. Chapters focus on marriage preparation, marriage enrichment, rebuilding troubled marriages, reconciling the separated, and working with stepfamilies, as well as how to organize a congregation for comprehensive marriage ministry. Materials from different "Marriage Saver Congregations" illustrate various approaches, and an extensive appendix contains sample brochures, letters, forms, and "Steps in Creating a Community Marriage Policy®."

Comprehensive Marriage and Family Ministry Organizations and Websites

Coalition for Marriage, Family, and Couples Education, LLC, *CMFCE@smartmarriages.com, www.smartmarriages.com*. This nondenominational, nonpartisan, nonsectarian organization offers the most comprehensive source of marriage and family ministry information and resources. For 14 years, ending in 2010, the Coalition held an annual Smart Marriages/Happy Families conference, bringing together researchers, program developers, and other experts for plenary sessions, seminars, workshops, and training institutes. At the website, you can order recordings of the presentations made at those conferences, read articles on a variety of relevant topics, check the Directory of Programs for available relationship education courses, and sign up for a free online e-newsletter.

Family Dynamics Institute. Contact Joshua Persall, Ministry Consultant, Family Dynamics Institute, 615-627-0751, *jpersall@familydynamics.net, www.familydynamics.net*. Family Dynamics Institute helps couples build strong marriages and families through inspiring classes, workshops, and education resources. Trained facilitators offer eight-week Dynamic Marriage classes through local churches. The Dynamic Marriage approach is very behavioral and experiential. Couples report great improvements, especially through praying together. "A New Beginning" is an intensive three-day workshop for couples in deep distress. Family Dynamics Ministry Consultants work with congregations to develop a Comprehensive Marriage Ministry to specifically address the needs of married couples at every age and stage of marriage.

Marriage Savers, Inc., 9311 Harrington Drive, Potomac, MD 20854. 301-469-5873, *Harriet@marriagesavers.org, www.marriagesavers.org*. Marriage Savers offers two-day seminars featuring national pioneers in the development of both Community Marriage Policies® and Marriage Savers Churches. In addition, whenever a Community Marriage Policy® is developed, Marriage Savers will train both clergy and lay mentor couples to create Marriage Savers Congregations. Webinar training events are offered as well, including online certification training for mentor couples and clergy for using the new customized version of the PREPARE-ENRICH premarital and marital inventories. Webinar dates and details are available at the website.

National Association for Relationship and Marriage Education (NARME). This organization champions the well-being of children through relationship and marriage education. Board directors are located across the United States, and the corporate office is located in Tallahassee, FL. Interested individuals or organizations can join NARME online and find information about annual conferences at the website, *http://www.narmeconference.com*.

Nonviolent Communication, PuddleDancer Press, PO Box 231129, Encinitas, CA 92023-1129, 858-759-6963, *www.nonviolentcommunication.com*. Nonviolent Communication, developed by Marshall Rosenburg in the 1960's, teaches people of all ages, genders, ethnicity, and background a more effective way to communicate. Separating observation from evaluation, taking responsibility for our feelings, making requests instead of demands, and listening empathically can enhance any relationship. Certified trainers now teach those skills all over the world. At the above website, you can sign up for an e-newsletter and other free resources, read articles about NVC, and purchase books (a basic text and companion workbook for group study and a variety of smaller books specifically addressed to parents, teachers, community leaders, etc. Also visit *www.cnvc.org/en/trainingcal* for more information, free introductory tools, upcoming events, and certified trainers. For telecourses, visit *www.nvctraining.com*.

The Association of Marriage and Family Ministries (AMFM), 8283 N. Hayden Rd., Suite 258, Scottsdale, AZ 85258, 480-718-3020, FAX: 480-718-3021, *staff@amfmonline.com, www.amfmonline.com, www.datenightevent.com*. AMFM's mission: "Impacting future generations by transforming marriages and families today." Operating out of a belief that "healthy marriages produce strong families, which create vibrant churches impacting their local communities and the world we live in for Christ," this ecumenical organization offers resources and events to train and equip the church for effective marriage and family ministry. Visit the websites to learn more about the various ministry teams, the annual Shift Conference, and the annual Marriage and Family Resource Guide.

United Methodist Marriage and Family Ministries: *www.gbod.org/marriage* and *www.gbod.org/family*. These websites offer a variety of helps for couples, pastors, and mentor couples: a directory of United Methodists trained in a variety of marriage and family programs; schedules of upcoming events and training opportunities; best practices articles; and annotated lists of marriage and family ministry organizations, curriculum resources, books and other publications recommended by United Methodists.

Resources for Relationship Education for Children, Youth, and Young Adults

Reading List for Relationship Education for Children, Youth, and Young Adults

9 Ways to Bring Out the Best in You and Your Child, by Maggie Reigh (Kelowna, Canada: Northstone Publishing, 2004, *www.northstone.com*). The author shows parents how to raise respectful, responsible, and resilient children, while bringing more life and laughter to their homes. Chapters focus on mutual respect, bringing values to life, mutual empowerment, dealing with feelings, effective communication, encouragement, living harmoniously, loving discipline, and helping children trust their inner guidance. This highly spiritual approach is presented in down-to-earth, easy-to-understand language with helpful examples of its application.

"Equipping Youth to Build Healthy Relationships," by Jane P. Ives, *www.gbod.org/marriage*. Web article formatted for download and distribution.

How to Avoid Falling in Love With a Jerk: The Foolproof Way to Follow Your Heart Without Losing Your Mind, by Dr. John Van Epp, Ph.D. (New York: McGraw-Hill, 2007) The author describes five dynamics that create the feelings of attachment in every relationship: knowledge, trust, reliance, commitment, and sexual touch. Understanding these dynamics can help persons avoid forming "over-attachments of the heart that override the judgments of the mind." Dr. Van Epp provides the following rule of thumb: "The degree or level of each bonding dynamic should never exceed the level of the previous." Individuals can learn to predict what a person will be like after marriage by thoroughly investigating five specific areas (family background, conscience, compatibility potential, relationship skills, past relationship patterns). Available through popular booksellers and at *www.lovethinks.com* (click on Singles and then PICK - Pick a Partner - for purchase of this book and related study course materials).

Living Together: Myths, Risks, and Answers, by Mike and Harriet McManus, (New York: Howard Books, 2008). The authors dispel the myth that living together leads to a successful marriage, exploring the risks as revealed by research and by their counseling experiences with couples. This book also provides helpful guidance for marriage preparation counseling.

The 7 Habits of Highly Effective Families: Building a Beautiful Family Culture in a Turbulent World, by Stephen R. Covey and Sandra M. Covey (NY: Golden Books, 1997), *http://www.franklincovey.com/ tc/solutions/home-and-family-solutions*. The authors show how establishing new patterns of thinking and doing can transform a family's relationships and life together, focusing on "7 habits": "Take responsibility for your life," "Define your mission and goals in life," "Prioritize, and do the most important things first," "Have an everyone-can-win attitude," "Listen to people sincerely," "Work together to achieve more,"

and "Renew yourself regularly." This framework for unconditional love, mutual respect, personal responsibility, and interdependence culminates in a process for mutual problem-solving. Each of the "7 habits" is presented clearly, with moving examples from real life, followed by guidelines for discussion with adults, teens, and/or children, providing an excellent study for a parenting class. [Available through popular booksellers and at the website above.]

The 7 Habits of Highly Effective Teens, by Sean Covey (NY: Fireside, 1998) and *The 7 Habits of Highly Effective Teens Workbook*, by Sean Covey (NY: Fireside, 2004), *http://www.franklincovey.com/ tc/solutions/home-and-family-solutions*. Stephen Covey's son presents the "7 habits" principles in language and with examples relevant to teenagers, excellent resources for individual or group study. Available through popular booksellers and at the website above.

What Children Learn From Their Parents' Marriage, by Judith P. Siegel, Ph.D., C.S.W. (New York: HarperCollins Publishers, 2000). Because the marriage relationship serves as the child's "blueprint for intimacy," couples need to discover how they have been impacted by the relationship of their parents and what they, in turn, are communicating to their children. Each chapter discusses and gives clear examples of an aspect of healthy intimacy: ("Establishing the Priority of the Marriage," "Teaching the Value of Interdependence," "Instilling the Importance of Mutual Respect," "Maintaining Trust in Word and Deed," "Negotiating Differences Constructively," "Understanding the Long-Term Effects of Conflict," "Emphasizing the Positives," "Building a Better Marriage." Questions at the end of each chapter encourage couples to reflect on their own relationships and to move toward healthier patterns both for their own happiness and for that of their children. This would be an excellent gift for individual couples or a resource for a nine-week group study for young parents.

Curriculum Materials for Relationship Education for Children, Youth, and Young Adults

Active Parenting Now, by Michael H. Popkin, Ph.D. (Active Parenting Publishers, Inc., 2002), Active Parenting Publishers, Inc., 1220 Kennestone Circle, Suite 130, Marietta, GA 30066, 800-825-

0060, *www.ActiveParenting.com*. This six-session curriculum for parents of children ages five to twelve provides excellent insights on "Winning Cooperation," teaching "Responsibility and Discipline," "Understanding and Redirecting Misbehavior," and "Building Courage, Character, and Self-Esteem." Family Enrichment Activities and Family Meeting suggestions strengthen families and the individuals in them. The Biblical and Theological Guide described below offers supplementary activities and materials for faith communities.

Active Parenting Now in the Faith Community: A Biblical and Theological Guide, by Freda Gardner (Atlanta: Active Parenting Publishers, 2003). The author provides general guidelines and specific suggestions, including handouts, for adapting the above program for faith communities.

Building Relationships: Developing Skills for Life, by David H. Olson, John DeFrain, and Amy K. Olson (Minneapolis, MN: Life Innovations, Inc., 1999) Each of the thirteen chapters focuses on one of the PREPARE/ENRICH categories and begins with a self-scoring quiz, which participants take before and after reading the chapter. The goal of this program is to help youth develop personal and relationship skills they can use throughout their lives: assertiveness, active listening, constructive conflict resolution, verbal and nonverbal communication, managing finances and creating a budget, finding and using a mentor, defining goals and taking steps to reach them. No training is required to use this resource. The student workbook and teacher's manual (with either PowerPoint or transparencies) may be purchased at *www.prepare-enrich.com* or from popular booksellers.

Created by God: Tweens, Faith, and Human Sexuality, New Edition, by James Ritchie (Nashville: Abingdon Press, 2010). This updated resource for fifth and sixth graders emphasizes a healthy biblical and Christian perspective on human sexuality, relationships, and values for "tweens." A Leader's Guide CD-ROM and a DVD provide guidance for planning, promotion, and leading the program. The Student Book and Parent Guide provide information for individual study, for parent-child discussion, and for classroom use. Other resources are listed in the back of the Parent Guide. Order through Cokesbury 800-672-1789 or *www.cokesbury.com*.

"Empowering Parents," by Jane P. Ives, *www.gbod.org/marriage*. Web article formatted for download and distribution.

Teen Sexuality Resources: Let's Be Real: Honest Discussions About Faith and Sexuality (Nashville: Abingdon, 1998). This leader's resource addresses issues related to youth sexuality and offers several models for learning experiences with youth grades 6 through 12. Purchase through Cokesbury, 800-672-1789 or *www.cokesbury.com*.

• *Let's Decide: Faith and My Sexuality* (Nashville: Abingdon, 2010). This student resource discusses beliefs, values, and sexuality, providing guidance for healthy decision-making.
• *Let's Listen: Communicating With Your Youth About Faith and Sexuality* (Nashville: Abingdon, 2010). This PDF electronic download for parents provides practical help and simple techniques for inviting conversation about faith and sexuality.

Ten Things Teens Should Know About Marriage (brochure), The Dibble Institute for Marriage Education, P.O. Box 7881, Berkeley, CA, 94707-0881, 800-695-7975, FAX: 510-649-5009, *Relationshipskills@DibbleInstitute.org, www.DibbleInstitute.org*. This brochure presents marriage as a beneficial goal for teens and offers ten tips to increase chances for a healthy, happy, long-term marriage. Order by phone or from the website: Click on "Bookstore," then on "Shop By - Media Type," then on "Brochures." Other selections available for youth and parents include *What You Should Know About Living Together, 50 Things Everyone Should Know About Dating Violence, 9 Signs of a Healthy Relationship, Relationship Redux: Tips and Scripts for Talking to Your Kids About Relationships*, and more. Purchase in bulk to share throughout your congregation and community.

The Connections Series, by Charlene R. Kamper (Berkley, California: The Dibble Institute for Marriage Education, 1996, 1999, 2004, 2010). These two complete ready-to-teach programs help teens learn skills essential for healthy, fulfilling relationships. Intended for use in schools, youth groups, and youth organizations, available in both religious and nonreligious language, the content is nonsexual and reflects current research in family life education. Effective teaching methods incorporate games and exercises to deepen understanding and strengthen skills. The complete kit for each course includes an Instructor's Manual, complete lesson plans for 15 one-hour sessions, transparency and handout masters, activity and game cards, and thirty student workbooks. Extra student workbooks and instructor's kits may be purchased. Free sample lessons available by request. *Dating and Emotions* (2010) helps thirteen- through seventeen-year-olds learn how relationships develop, how to communicate effectively, how to spot destructive patterns, how to deal with emotions, and other interpersonal skills. *Relationships and Marriage* (1996), for young adults ages sixteen through twenty, gives participants practical tools for understanding, managing, and making wise decisions about their relationships. Order from The Dibble Institute for Marriage Education, P.O. Box 7881, Berkeley, California, 94707-0881, 800-695-7975, FAX: 510-649-5009, *Relationshipskills@DibbleInstitute.org, www.DibbleInstitute.org.*

The LoveU2 Series, by Marline F. Pearson (Berkeley, CA: The Dibble Institute for Marriage Education, 2004), 800-695-7975, *RelationshipSkills@DibbleInstitute.org, www.DibbleInstitute.org* . These activity-based courses may be used separately or in sequence or in combination, by using key lessons from each. Designed for use in public settings, these materials are completely compatible with Christian teachings and easily adapted by adding worship moments before, during, and/or after sessions. Course titles: *Baby Smarts: Through the Eyes of a Child; Becoming Sex Smart; Communication Smarts for All Relationships; Dating Smarts: A Bit More Than Friends for Younger Teens; Relationship Smarts Plus*. Sample lessons are available at the website.

Things to Know Before You Say "Go": Powerful Questions to Ask Before You Give Your Heart Away, Elizabeth Martindale, Psy.D. (2009, *www.couragetobloom.com*). This attractively packaged set contains 76 question cards for individuals to ask themselves to evaluate a potential or actual dating partner. The accompanying booklet explains the importance of consciousness in dating and relationships and provides instructions for various card sort and discussion activities. Sample questions: "Can this person accept things about me I am unable or unwilling to change? 'How does this person deal with disappointment and loss?" "Do I like how this person responds when I am hurting or upset?" "Does this person follow through on commitments and obligations?" The cards may also be used for self-evaluation and for clarification of priorities. Also available from the Dibble Institute, 800-695-7975, *RelationshipSkills@DibbleInstitute.org, www.DibbleInstitute.org.*

What's Reel? Myths and Facts About Marriage, (Berkeley, CA: The Dibble Institute for Marriage Education, 2010), 800-695-7975, *RelationshipSkills@DibbleInstitute.org, www.DibbleInstitute.org*. The vast majority of teens say that marriage and family are a high priority for their future, but most youthful ideas about marriage reflect not facts, but media messages, street talk, and poor role models. Using popular movies, *What's Reel?* provides seven ready-to-teach and fun lessons to help teens compare ideas about marriage with actual research, examine their own expectations, become critical observers of media, and identify helpful and problematic behaviors.

Organizations and Websites for Relationship Education for Children, Youth, and Young Adults

The Dibble Institute for Marriage Education, P.O. Box 7881, Berkeley, CA, 94707-0881, 800-695-7975, FAX: 510-649-5009, *Relationshipskills@DibbleInstitute.org, www.DibbleInstitute.org*. "The Dibble Institute equips young people with the skills and knowledge they need to develop healthy romantic relationships now and in the future. We will be successful when more children are nurtured and protected by their own parents in a healthy marriage and when more young people make healthy life choices." The website offers curriculum resources and training opportunities for workers with youth. You can order helpful brochures for teens and sign up for monthly e-newsletters to keep abreast of new research and resources. A link to www.stayteen.org provides teens with information about relationships and sex in an attractive and fun format, including interactive quizzes and games.

Resources for Marriage Preparation Ministries

Reading List for Marriage Preparation Ministries

All-in-One Marriage Prep: 75 Experts Share Tips and Wisdom to Help You Get Ready Now, by Susanne M. Alexander (Naples, FL: Barringer, 2010). This comprehensive collection of short articles by various authors is grouped by topic and covers a wide-range of issues for courting, engaged, and newlywed couples to consider and discuss. Contributors include Claudia and David Arp, John Van Epp, Mark Gungor, Scott Haltzman, Mike McManus, and others. Marriage Transformation L.L.C., 800-501-6682, *www.allinonemarriageprep.com.*

Before You Remarry: A Guide to Successful Remarriage, by H. Norman Wright (Eugene, Oregon: Harvest House, 1999). This workbook, for couples in which one or both have been previously married, promotes interaction on the major issues of marriage, including making sure they are ready to marry again. Couples discover how to use positive experiences from previous marriages and how to overcome the negative, along with how to handle common problems related to previous and new in-laws, blended families, financial concerns, and sexual issues. Available through popular booksellers or Cokesbury (800-672-1789) or *www.cokesbury.com.*

Before You Say "I Do," by H. Norman Wright and Wes Roberts (Eugene, Oregon: Harvest House, 1997). This workbook provides interactive surveys, thoughtful questions, and real-life examples to help couples discover areas of harmony and areas of potential discord. Couples can deepen their relationship by exploring ways to adjust to their differences, clarifying role expectations, developing spiritual intimacy, establishing a healthy sexual relationship, handling finances, and building healthy relationships with in-laws. Available through popular booksellers or Cokesbury (800-672-1789) or *www.cokesbury.com.*

"Best Practices in Marriage Preparation," by Jane P. Ives, *www.gbod.org/marriage.* Web article formatted for download and distribution.

Mixed Matches: How to Create successful Interracial, Interethnic, and Interfaith Relationships, by Joel Crohn, Ph.D. (New York: Fawcett Columbine, 1995). The author, drawing on years of counseling experience, shows couples in cross-cultural relationships how to approach each other compassionately and negotiate solutions to their cultural and religious differences. This book also offers practical advice on how couples can confront prejudice, deal with in-laws, and help their children develop a sense of identity in a bicultural family.

Take Back Your Wedding: Managing the People Stress of Wedding Planning, by William J. Doherty, PhD. and Elizabeth Doherty Thomas (2007), *www.thefirstdance.com.* The authors address various wedding planning issues, providing resources and sound advice for dealing with them in ways that strengthen family relationships and prevent future problems.

Things I Wish I'd Known Before We Got Married, by Gary Chapman (Chicago: Northfield Publishing, 2010). The author's practical wisdom and tips dispel the myths, illusions, and expectations that can undermine happiness in marriage. This would be an excellent gift for engaged or newlywed couples.

Curriculum Materials and Other Resources for Marriage Preparation Ministries

Christian Weddings: Resources to Make Your Ceremony Unique, Revised Edition, by Andy Langford (Nashville: Abingdon Press, 2008). Couples can personalize their wedding ceremonies by selecting liturgical elements from an expanded range of resources. The enclosed CD-ROM facilitates choosing different elements and arranging them into a single service.

GROWING LOVE IN CHRISTIAN MARRIAGE Couple's Edition, by Richard and Joan Hunt (Nashville: Abingdon Press, 2001). For use by couples for marriage preparation, pre-wedding counseling, and marriage counseling, with a pastor, mentor couple, or independently. The Couple's Edition provides information, suggestions, discussion exercises, Scripture, and excerpts from the Service of Christian Marriage. The Couple's Edition is organized around four vital marriage themes from I Corinthians 13: "Faith Through Covenantal Commitment" (what each person brings to the marriage); "Hope as Vision for Your Journey" (goals, transitions, challenges and opportunities for growth); "Love Through Daily Caring Relationships" (the couple, their families, and their work); "Power Through Shared Communication" (basic skills for communication in marriage). Sixty "Explore" guides and a "Marriage Lifestyle Questionnaire" help identify strengths and areas for growth. Additional helps for using the Couple's Edition are provided in the companion piece, the GROWING LOVE IN CHRISTIAN MARRIAGE Pastor's Manual.

Interfaith Wedding Ceremonies: Samples and Sources, selected and with an introduction by Joan C. Hawxhurst (Kalamazoo, MI: Dovetail Publishing, 1996). The author discusses issues interfaith couples should consider when planning their wedding, then offers sample ceremonies, excerpts from other ceremonies, and a variety of helpful resources.

Marriage Mentoring: Twelve Conversations, by Dr. Edward A. Gray, LMFT(2005). Training and discussion guides for twelve mentoring sessions with engaged couples or newlyweds. These sessions are based on sharing of personal stories and experiences around twelve specific topics in order to build a supportive relationship and help couples approach marriage with realistic expectations and practical information. For more information or to purchase, call 901-681-9200 or contact *egray@harding.edu, www.12conversations.com*. Visit the website to learn about other 12 Conversation programs, including an international version and programs specifically designed for dating couples, military couples, senior citizens, and caregivers.

Saving Your Marriage Before It Starts: Seven Questions to Ask Before—and After—You Marry, by Dr. Les Parrott III and Dr. Leslie Parrott (Grand Rapids, Michigan: Zondervan Publishing House, 2006), *www.zondervan.com*. This kit includes a hardcover copy of *Saving Your Marriage Before It Starts*, leader's guide, one men's and one women's workbook (each containing a self-test), and a nine-session DVD presentation by the authors. Each participating couple needs one each of the men's workbook, women's workbook, and the hardcover book. Churches may order by calling 800-727-3480; individuals may order from the website.

Premarital Inventories

FOCCUS: Facilitating Open Couple Communication, Understanding, and Study, (Omaha, Nebraska: FOCCUS Inc. USA, 1985, 1997, 2000, 2010). Nazareth Hall, 3300 North 60th Street, Omaha, NE 68104 (402-827-3735), *focus@focusinc.com, www.foccusinc.com*. This inventory provides individualized couple feedback on where each partner stands in regard to topics important to marriage. It is not a predictor of marital success or failure, but a tool to help couples communicate and work through issues before marriage. The inventory can be administered to an individual couple or to groups, but discussion and feedback should take place privately with each couple. The act of responding to the questions raises issues for the couple to discuss, even before it is scored. Forms are scored online by the facilitator, using the QuickScore, or the facilitator can arrange for the couple to take the inventory on line. A facilitator uses the report analyzing the couple's responses to help them reflect on the following topics: Life-

Style Expectations, Friends and Interests, Personality Match, Personal Issues, Communication, Problem-Solving, Religion and Values, Parenting Issues, Extended Family Issues, Sexuality Issues, Financial Issues, Readiness Issues, Marriage Covenant, Key Problem Indicators, Family of Origin, and Dual Careers. Additional questions are available for the following topics, where appropriate: Interfaith Marriages, Second Marriages, and Cohabiting Couples. FOCCUS is available in English, Spanish, French Canadian, Korean, Chinese, and Portuguese; as well as in six different versions: Catholic, Christian non-denominational, General, Orthodox Christian, Alternate, and Spanish Abridged (for lower reading levels or disabled persons). Training is required and may be done online or with a certified FOCCUS© Trainer.

"Marriage Lifestyle Questionnaire," in the GROWING LOVE IN CHRISTIAN MARRIAGE Couple's Manual, by Richard and Joan Hunt (Nashville: United Methodist Publishing House, 2000). Instructions for administering and interpreting this Inventory are provided in this GROWING LOVE IN CHRISTIAN MARRIAGE Pastor's Manual, by Cliff and Jane Ives, same publisher.

Premarriage Awareness Inventory, by Peter L. Velander (St. Paul, MN: Logos Productions Inc., 1993). Recognizing that couples coming to be married are increasing likely to be cohabiting or remarrying, the author developed this resource to enable pastors to address nonjudgmentally the impact of these factors on a relationship. Available in three versions: First Time (also available in an online version), Remarriage, and Cohabitation. *The Counseling Packet* includes multiple-choice surveys for each participant and a Profile Copy for compiling the individual responses on a single form for comparison and discussion. *The Administrator's Portfolio* provides clear information about administering, evaluating, and using the inventory in pre-marital counseling with couples. *A Good Beginning* is an optional 46-page resource for couples to read on their own. Reading assignments are suggested in *The Administrator's Portfolio*, which outlines four counseling sessions. Contact Logos Productions, Inc., P.O. Box 240, South St. Paul, MN 55075-0240, 800-328-0200, or visit *www.logosproductions.com*.

PREPARE/ENRICH is a scientifically validated relationship inventory and program that helps dating, engaged, and married couples discuss and understand their relationship while learning valuable relationship skills. The online Customized Version makes it easy for couples to complete the inventory, with content tailored to their relationship stage and structure. Within minutes after a couple have completed the online Customized Version of PREPARE/ENRICH, the Facilitator may view or print a 25-page Facilitator's Report and ten-page Couple Report, along with resources to help with the feedback process, including a Couple's Workbook. Certification training is required to become a PREPARE/ENRICH Facilitator, and upon completion a Facilitator ID number is issued along with materials and a complimentary scoring credit. The online version is available in English, French, German, Korean, Spanish, and Swiss, The older paper and pencil version is available in Chinese, English, and Spanish. Contact PREPARE/ENRICH at *www.prepare-enrich.com* or 800-331-1661 for more information and/or to find a certification workshop or trainer near you.

Marriage Preparation Ministry Organizations and Websites

Engaged Encounter United Methodist, *www.encounter.org*. This organization offers weekend experiences for engaged couples, providing an opportunity for private reflection and discussion of their dreams, ambitions, and attitudes. To find dates and locations for Engaged Encounter United Methodist events, visit the website or call 866-633-3862.

www.thefirstdance.com: This website provides resources for marriage preparation and wedding planning. Articles address both couple and extended family dynamics, showing how to deal with a variety of issues in ways that prevent future problems.

Resources for Marriage Education and Enrichment Ministries

Marriage Education and Enrichment Reading List

Adult Children of Divorced Parents: Making Your Marriage Work, by Beverly and Tom Rodgers (San Jose, CA: Resource Publications, Inc., 2002). Adult children of divorced parents can overcome the negative effects of that experience and improve the odds of marital success by understanding their wounds,

breaking out of reactivity patterns, and learning how to help each other heal. The authors write out of their own experience as well as that of couples with whom they have worked, offering Scripture-based insights and exercises.

A Joyful Meeting: Sexuality in Marriage, by Drs. Mike and Joyce Grace (St. Paul, Minnesota: International Marriage Encounter, 1980). The authors discuss marital sexuality both from a spiritual viewpoint and with humor. They emphasize the importance of mature love for sexual harmony and share practical advice for overcoming the conflicts that are likely to arise because of sexual differences.

A Lasting Promise: A Christian Guide to Fighting for Your Marriage, by Scott Stanley, Daniel Trathen, Savanna McCain, and Milt Bryan (San Francisco: Jossey-Bass Publishers, 1998). The relationship principles of PREP (Prevention and Enhancement Program), are linked to Scripture in this book. Based on solid research, this work shows couples how they can make their marriages stronger and happier. *Fighting For Your Marriage*, by the same authors, presents the same concepts in secular language.

And They Were Not Ashamed: Strengthening Marriage Through Sexual Fulfillment, by Laura M. Brotherson (Boise, Idaho: Inspire Book, 2004). "As three books in one, this marriage book, sex book and parenting book: Shines light and truth on the intimate marital relationship, restoring sex to its proper position as ordained of God; Effectively addresses, with self-help solutions, the emotional, spiritual and physical intimacy issues that plague so many marriages; Provides principles and practices to help parents teach and better prepare their children for intimacy and lasting fulfillment in marriage" (back cover).

"Couple Relationships and Money Issues," by Jane P. Ives, www.gbod.org/marriage, web-article formatted for download and distribution.

Couples and the Art of Playing: Three Easy and Enjoyable Ways to Nurture and Heal Relationships, by Keith Hackett (Lincoln, Nebraska: iUniverse, Inc., 2003). The author, a United Methodist pastor and Marriage and Family Therapist, encourages couples to develop playful, creative habits to enrich and strengthen their marriages.

Empowering Couples: Building on Your Strengths, by David H. Olson and Amy K. Olson (Minneapolis, MN: Life Innovations, Inc., 2000). Each chapter begins with a quiz about a particular relationship topic to help couples or individuals assess their strengths and needs for growth in that area. Clarifying information is followed by couple exercises to help turn "stumbling blocks into stepping stones" (p. ix).

Foundations Newsletter for Newly Married Couples, by Steve and Kathy Beirne (Portland, ME: S&K Publishers, *www.facetsite.com/foundations/about.html*). This bimonthly newsletter addresses different marriage relationship topics in each issue. Bulk rates are available for pastors who wish to buy subscriptions for couples they have married.

Getting the Love You Want: A Guide for Couples, by Harville Hendrix, Ph.D. (New York: Harper and Row, Publishers, Inc., 2008). This classic work describes the unconscious needs which lead us to choose our mates and how learned behaviors from childhood lead to conflict; shows how to learn positive ways to meet those needs; and outlines a ten-week course in relationship therapy couples can do on their own.

His Needs, Her Needs: Building An Affair-Proof Marriage, by Willard F. Harley, Jr. (Grand Rapids, Michigan: Fleming H. Revell, 2011). Based on the simple premise that husbands and wives can find lifelong happiness in marriage by committing themselves to meet each other's needs, this book offers information and exercises to help couples deepen their understanding of each other and intentionally behave in ways that will nourish the relationship. The author explains that with every encounter we affect each other positively or negatively, making deposits in or withdrawals from each other's "Love Bank." The author also clarifies the dynamics that may make spouses vulnerable to the temptation of an affair and offers strategies for healing relationships damaged by infidelity.

Hold Me Tight: Seven Conversations for a Lifetime of Love, by Sue Johnson (New York: Little, Brown, & Company, 2008). This easy-to-understand and practical guide for couples stresses the importance of emotional attachment. The seven transforming conversations, which encourage the emotional responsiveness vital to healthy, lasting marriages, help couples recognize destructive dialogue patterns, find their emotional "raw spots," revisit rocky moments, communicate needs, connect and engage with each other, forgive and repair injuries, bond through sex and touch, and keep their love alive.

How One of You Can Bring the Two of You Together: Breakthrough Strategies to Resolve Your Conflicts and Reignite Your Love, by Susan Page (NY: Broadway Books, 1997, *www.susanpage.com*).

The author's insights and suggestions will help both those who feel stuck and frustrated with their relationships and those who, although happy and stable, feel some disillusionment or lack of connection. Page presents eight "experiments" which one person can implement: 1) Act on your own. 2) Do the opposite of what you have been doing. 3) Reframe a power struggle. 4) Enlist your partner's help. 5) Express empathy for your partner's position. 6) Gracefully accept what you can't change. 7) Ask for what you want. 8) Men: tune in; Women: stop coaching.

Intended for Pleasure: Sex Technique and Sexual Fulfillment in Christian Marriage, by Ed Wheat, M.D., and Gaye Wheat (Grand Rapids, Michigan: Fleming H. Revell, 2010). The authors provide comprehensive and clear information about many aspects of sex and sexuality from a Christian perspective: understanding the basics, techniques of lovemaking, solutions to common problems, and suggestions for specific situations such as pregnancy and aging.

Keeping the Love You Find: A Personal Guide, by Harville Hendrix, Ph.D. (New York: Atria Books, 1992). The author provides information and exercises to help readers deepen their understanding of who they are and what they long for in their relationships, then to learn the skills to make behavior changes needed in order to achieve an intentional, "conscious" relationship.

Love and Anger in Marriage, by David Mace (Grand Rapids, Michigan: Zondervan Publishing House, 1982). Couples can learn to accept anger as a normal function of relationship, to communicate without attacking each other, and to work together for positive solutions to whatever produces the anger in the first place. Available at *www.bettermarriages.org*.

Love & Respect: The Love She Most Desires, The Respect He Desperately Needs, by Emerson Eggerichs, (Colorado Springs: Integrity Publishers, 2004). Writing from a Christian perspective and frequently quoting Scripture, the author makes a clear case for the importance of honoring the primary needs of women and men. He identifies the "Crazy Cycle" (she reacts to a perceived lack of love and he reacts to a perceived lack of respect) and recommends clear steps to move toward closeness and a mutually satisfying relationship.

Love Is Never Enough, by Aaron T. Beck, M.D. (New York: Harper & Row, Publishers, 1988). The author explores how couples can avoid the misunderstandings and inaccurate interpretations of each other's behavior that lead to marital conflict. This book shows partners how "to be more reasonable with each other by adopting a more humble, tentative attitude about the accuracy of their mind reading, and its resulting negative conclusions; by checking out the accuracy of their mind reading; and by considering alternative explanations for what a partner does" (p. 17).

Love, Marriage, and Money: Understanding and Achieving Financial Compatibility Before-and-After-You Say "I Do," by Gail Liberman and Alan Lavine (Lincoln, NE: iUniverse, Inc., 2005). The authors blend psychological, legal, and financial information into a helpful resource for couples. Topics include financial personalities, how to compromise, renting or purchasing a home, planning for children, preparing for retirement, and estate planning.

Passages of Marriage: Five Growth Stages That Take your Marriage to Greater Intimacy and Fulfillment, by Dr. Frank and Mary Alice Minirth, Dr. Brian and Dr. Deborah Newman, and Dr. Robert and Susan Hemfelt (Nashville: Thomas Nelson, Inc., 1991). These authors discuss five stages of marriage: Young Love, Realistic Love, Comfortable Love, Renewing Love, and Transcendent Love. The tasks of each stage are clearly described, with suggestions and self-assessment exercises to help couples make the most of each passage.

Sacred Marriage: What if God Designed Marriage to Make Us Holy More Than to Make Us Happy? by Gary Thomas (Grand Rapids, MI: Zondervan Publishing House, 2000). The author invites readers to view marriage as a spiritual discipline through which persons can come to know God more fully and intimately. Marriage teaches us to love and to respect others, exposes our sin, and encourages us to develop perseverance, forgiveness, and the ability to embrace differences.

The Dance of Anger: A Woman's Guide to Changing the Patterns of Intimate Relationships, by Harriet Goldhor Lerner, Ph.D. (New York: Harper & Row, Publishers, 1997). "Close relationships are akin to circular dances, in which the behavior of each partner provokes and maintains the behavior of the other" (p. 12). This book helps the reader clarify her feelings, learn to communicate them effectively, and interrupt negative patterns in relationships, not only with her husband, but also with children, parents, and others.

The Five Love Languages: How to Express Heartfelt Commitment to Your Mate, by Gary Chapman (Chicago: Northfield Publishing, 1992). The author identifies five languages of love: Quality Time, Words of Affirmation, Gifts, Acts of Service, and Physical Touch. By learning to speak and understand these unique languages, persons can more effectively communicate love and feel more truly loved as well.

The Gift of Sex: A Christian Guide to Sexual Fulfillment, by Clifford and Joyce Penner (Waco, Texas: Word, Inc., 2003). The book offers detailed information on the physical, emotional, and spiritual dimensions of sexual relationships. It provides a biblical perspective, advice for moving past sexual barriers and resolving difficulties, and sexual enhancement exercises for increasing awareness and pleasure.

The Love Dare, by Stephen Kendrick and Alan Kendrick (Nashville, TN: B&H Publishing Group, 2008). Based on the book featured in the movie *Fireproof*, this book offers forty days of faith-based relationship information and challenges to be used by a spouse hoping to improve his or her marriage.

The Secrets of Happily Married Men: Eight Ways to Win Your Wife's Heart Forever, by Scott Haltzman, M.D. with Theresa Foy Digeronimo (San Francisco, CA:Jossey-Bass, 2006). The author shows men how to use their natural masculine talents to enhance their marriages. The determination to do a job and to do it right (focusing, prioritizing, developing strategies, problem-solving, paying attention to details, negotiating and compromising, resolving conflict, working through step-by-step processes, and achieving goals) can be used to build a strong, healthy, and lasting marriage.

You Just Don't Understand: Women and Men in Conversation, by Deborah Tannen, Ph.D. (New York, Ballentine Books, 1990). The author analyzes how boys and girls develop different perspectives and communication styles because of differences in how they are raised. By trying to see things from the other's perspective, rather than reacting negatively, men and women can prevent these differences from undermining their relationships.

"Why Marriage Education and Enrichment?" by Jane P. Ives, *www.gbod.org/marriage*. Web article formatted for download and distribution.

Why Marriages Succeed or Fail: What You Can Learn From the Breakthrough Research to Make Your Marriage Last, by John Gottman, Ph.D. with Nan Silver (New York: Simon & Schuster, 1994). The author presents four strategies for breaking cycles of negativity and maintaining a lasting, healthy marriage: calming yourself so that you are not overwhelmed by flooding emotions, speaking and listening nondefensively, validating each other as well as your relationship, and overlearning these principles so that the new skills become automatic and can be used under stress.

Why Mars and Venus Collide: Improving Relationships by Understanding How Men and Women Cope Differently With Stress, by John Gray, Ph.D, (New York: Harper, 2008). The author explains male/female differences, drawing on brain scan and hormone research to clarify how men and women react differently to stress and often misunderstand each other. He offers clear, concrete steps to prevent and heal the conflicts that arise from such misunderstandings.

Why Talking Is Not Enough: Eight Loving Actions that Will Transform Your Marriage, by Susan Page (San Francisco: Jossey-Bass, A Wiley Imprint, 2006). The author encourages individuals and couples to treat their relationships as spiritual disciplines, practicing acceptance, compassion, restraint, and kindness. By focusing on loving each other, in a spirit of good will, couples can build a true spiritual partnership. The author's insights and "experiments" can be utilized by both or by just one party in the relationship.

Devotional Resources for Couples

15-Minute Devotions for Couples, by Bob and Emilie Barnes (Eugene, Oregon: Harvest House Publishers, 1995). Brief selections offer Scripture passages, related devotional reading, and suggestions for activities to strengthen couple communication and intimacy.

365 Meditations for Couples, edited by Sally D. Sharpe (Nashville: Dimensions for Living, 2003). Daily selections offer Scripture, a brief meditation, prayer, and a "Talk It Over" topic for couples. Each month's selections are written by a different couple.

Couples' Devotional Bible: New International Version, (Grand Rapids, Michigan: Zondervan Publishing House, 2009). In addition to the complete text of the Bible, this volume offers helpful introductions to each book, daily devotions with "marriage builder" activities, and other helps for exploring various areas of your marriage. An index helps locate devotional readings on specific topics with which couples might need assistance.

Holy Relationships, by Christine A. Adams (Harrisburg, Pennsylvania: Morehouse Publishing, 1998). Approximately eighty-five brief paragraphs and Scripture passages for daily readings are grouped under three headings: "Guidelines for Holy Relationships," "Practices of Holy Relationships," and "Purposes of Holy Relationships." Topics include forgiveness, feelings, autonomy, listening, faith, developing rituals, affirming your love, and more.

In the Presence of God: Readings for a Christian Marriage, by David and Vera Mace (Philadelphia: The Westminster Press, 1985). Four weeks worth of daily meditations on "The Purposes of Marriage," "The Adjustments of Marriage," "The Fellowship of Marriage," and "The Wider Implications of Marriage." Each entry includes Scripture, quotations and reflections, and prayer. Available at *www.bettermarriages.org*.

Program Guides and Curriculum Resources for Marriage Education and Enrichment

10 Great Dates to Energize Your Marriage Video Kit, by Claudia and David Arp (Grand Rapids, Michigan: Zondervan Publishing House, 1997). This kit contains two 75-minute videos, featuring ten fun date launches, a Leader's Guide, and one Participant's Book, which includes a dating guide with tear-out sheets. Couples come together for the video date launch with its low-key discussion starter; then each couple has time alone to talk during their date. The program could be scheduled one night a week for ten weeks, one night every other week or once a month, or over the course of a weekend retreat. You will need one copy of the *10 Great Dates* book for each participating couple. Order through Marriage Alive International, Inc., P.O. Box 31408, Knoxville, TN 37930, 888-690-6667, *www.marriagealive.com*, *mailine97@aol.com*. Also available through popular booksellers and Cokesbury, 800-672-1789 or *www.cokesbury.com*.

Building Lasting Marriages: A Study Guide for Marriage Enrichment, by Dr. Bobbye Wood (Fort Worth, TX: Britton Wood & Associates, 2002, 2004). The author uses personal examples and humor in nine study sessions with exercises for couples based on Better Marriages (formerly Association for Couples in Marriage Enrichment) principles and the work of David and Vera Mace. This book would work well for a Marriage Enrichment Group. Available at *www. bettermarriages.org*.

Fireproof Your Marriage: Couple's Kit, by Jennifer Dion (Vista, CA: Outreach, Inc., 2008), 800-991-6011, *www.outreach.com*. This kit contains a six-session DVD and two copies of the Participant's Guide. The DVD sessions recap briefly (2-5 minutes each) scenes from the Fireproof movie. The Participant's Guide provides discussion questions, Scripture references, and exercises for use by couples or small groups. The movie itself is available through video/ DVD rental sources, but a special license is required for public showings, other than in a private home. You may purchase the license, which is good for one year, by visiting *www.cvli.com* or calling 800-991-6011. The cost of the site license, which underwrites Christian filmmaking, is based on average church attendance (for an average worship attendance of 95, the license costs $99.).

Get Going and Grow: An Eight-month MEG Curriculum Leaders' Manual (Better Marriages, 502 North Broad St., P.O. Box 21374, Winston-Salem, NC 27120, 336-724-1526, 800-634-8325, *info@bettermarriages.org, www.bettermarriages.org*). The Leaders' Manual provides guidance for establishing and leading a Marriage Enrichment Group (MEG) and all materials needed for eight months of meetings.

Making Love Last a Lifetime: Biblical Perspectives on Love, Marriage, and Sex, by Adam Hamilton (Nashville: Abingdon, 2004). This kit contains a Leader's Guide, DVD, participant's book, and other helps for an eight-week series for married couples of all ages or for singles or couples preparing for marriage. A Pastor's Guide with CD-ROM provides directions for a church-wide emphasis and community outreach using this program. Order through Cokesbury, 800-672-1789 or *www.cokesbury.com*.

Money Habitudes: Target Your Habits and Attitudes About Money, created by Syble Solomon, (LifeWise, 2006, *www.moneyhabitudes.com*, 888-833-4331). This set of cards may be used by couples on their own or as part of a group activity to help persons determine the values and attitudes that guide their thoughts and actions in regard to saving, spending, and dealing with debt and money in general. Following the card sorting activity, participants discover the challenges and advantages of each financial type (Spontaneous, Status, Giving, Security, Carefree, and Planning) and learn ways to achieve

a healthy balance. Since differences in attitudes toward and use of money often cause conflict in marriage, couples benefit by increased understanding of themselves and each other and by learning to discuss their differences and make mutually agreeable decisions that take those differences into consideration. Also available in Spanish.

Right Steps: Discovering a Better Marriage (A Self-Guided Course for Couples and Leaders' Manual for group sessions), Winston-Salem, NC: The Association for Couples in Marriage Enrichment (now Better Marriages, 2006), 800-634-8325, *www. bettermarriages.org*. Clear directions and all materials needed for four two-hour sessions for couples to use by themselves or for leader couples to use with a group (adaptable to shorter time frames or for a retreat setting).

The Marriage Course, *www.themarriagecourseusa.org/m/*. Using this program, similar in format to the Alpha series, churches offer couples seven candlelit dinners, with a lively, often humorous video presentation at each, time to talk privately as a couple, and opportunity to practice new strategies to deepen their relationship. The Marriage Course is designed for couples who have good marriages and want to keep them that way, and it also helps couples get back to being happy when they've forgotten how. Order the Starter Kit, with videos, a leader's guide, and manuals for participating couples, at *http://www. alpharesources.org/stores/1/index.cfm*. Alpha also offers the Marriage Preparation Course, the Parenting Children Course, and the Parenting Teenagers Course.

The Second Half of Marriage: Facing the Eight Challenges of the Empty Nest Years DVD Curriculum (Zondervan Groupware), by Claudia and David Arp, MSW (Grand Rapids, Michigan: Zondervan Publishing House, 2000). Designed for a nine-session small group experience or weekend event, this kit includes a DVD and a Participant's Guide and a Leader's Guide, both of which may be purchased separately. Drawing on their national survey of hundreds of "second-half" couples, the Arps offer strategies for meeting each of the eight challenges of the empty nest years: letting go of past disappointments; creating a partner-focused rather than child-focused marriage; learning to communicate better; using anger and conflict in a creative, constructive way; building a deeper friendship; renewing romance; adjusting to changing roles with aging parents and adult children; growing closer to God and to each other. Order through Marriage Alive International, Inc., P.O. Box 31408, Knoxville, TN 37930, 888-690-6667, *www.marriagealive.com*.

Organizations and Websites for Marriage Education and Enrichment

Better Marriages (Association for Couples in Marriage Enrichment [ACME]), 502 North Broad Street, P.O. Box 21374, Winston-Salem, NC 27120, 336-724-1526, 800-634-8325, *acme@bettermarriages. org*, *www.bettermarriages.com*. Better Marriages is a nonprofit, nonsectarian organization promoting enrichment opportunities and resources to "strengthen couple relationships and enhance personal growth, mutual fulfillment and family wellness." Better Marriages focuses mainly on helping couples in good marriages achieve their full potential. A leadership training and certification program provides skills for leading various couple events. Call the office or visit the website to find out about leader couples and events in your area and to sign up for quarterly e-newsletters.

Imago Relationships International, *www.gettingtheloveyouwant.com*. Based on the work of Harville Hendrix and Helen LaKelly Hunt, this program offers books, workshops, and curriculum materials featuring the IMAGO dialogue process, which helps couples share thoughts and feelings in a way that can heal and nurture relationships. This process works effectively in all relationships, but is especially helpful for developing intimacy that can help heal childhood wounds. Visit the website to locate trainers and events near you.

Marriage Encounter/Engaged Encounter United Methodist (an Affiliate Organization with the United Methodist General Board of Discipleship), *www. encounter.org*. One of the twelve faith expressions of Worldwide Marriage Encounter, ME/EEUM offers Christian weekend experiences for couples who want to prepare for or enrich their marriages. A team of lay couples and a clergy-spouse couple make a series of presentations encouraging participants to look at themselves as individuals, at their relationship with each other, and at their relationship with God, the church, and the world. Following each presentation, couples are given time in the privacy of their own rooms for personal sharing using the techniques taught during the weekend. No group discussion is required. Post-weekend experiences for nurturing ongoing growth are offered in many local areas. Visit the website above to find events scheduled for your area. Visit *www.wwme.org* or call 800-795-5683 to learn more about Worldwide Marriage Encounter and other faith expressions of this ministry.

Resources for Ministries With Families in Special Situations, Transition, and Crisis

Reading List for Ministries With Families in Special Situations, Transition, and Crisis

Counseling Couples in Conflict: A Relational Restoration Model, by James N. Sells and Mark A. Yarhouse (Downers Grove, IL: InterVarsity Press, 2011). In this comprehensive resource for pastors and counselors, the authors integrate biblical principles, counseling skills, and theory to provide helpful understanding of marital conflict in general and in regard to such specific issues as addictions, sexual differences, infidelity, divorce, and blended families.

Divorce Busting: A Step-by-Step Approach to Making Your Marriage Loving Again, by Michele Weiner-Davis (New York: Simon & Schuster, 1992). The practical problem-solving approach in this book demonstrates how behavior change, even by just one partner, can improve the dynamics of a marriage relationship. The author's emphasis on finding solutions rather than exploring problems is based on a simple formula: "Do more of what works and less of what doesn't" (page 17).

Domestic Violence: What Every Pastor Needs to Know, by Reverend Al Miles (Minneapolis, Minnesota: Augsburg Fortress, 2011). The author explores the complex problem of domestic violence and offers guidance for ministering effectively with both perpetrators and victims. Warning pastors of the dangers inherent in naïve and untrained approaches to such situations, Miles makes a strong case for referrals to trained professionals and for all pastors to take part in domestic violence prevention training. Miles helps pastors see how they may inadvertently encourage and excuse violent behavior, while at the same time blaming the victims. He also recommends specific strategies for ensuring the safety of victims and for holding their abusers accountable. Available through popular booksellers and Cokesbury, 800-672-1789 or *www.cokesbury.com*.

"Facing Up to Pornography and Sexual Addictions," by Jane P. Ives, *www.gbod.org/marriage*. Web article formatted for download and distribution.

Grace and Divorce: God's Healing Gift to Those Whose Marriages Fall Short, by Dr. Les Carter (San Francisco: Jossey Bass, 2005). The author encourages both those who divorce and those who know and love them to remember that Jesus approached with compassion those who fall short of the highest standard of perfection. "My bias leans toward erring in the direction of maintaining the marriage if at all possible. At the same time, when people…tell me they've done all they can to save a marriage but to no avail, I want to be known as loving even if they divorce."

"Infidelity Prevention and Recovery," by Jane P. Ives, *www.gbod.org/marriage*. Web article formatted for download and distribution.

Not "Just Friends": Rebuilding Trust and Recovering Your Sanity After Infidelity, by Shirley P. Glass, Ph.D. with Jean Coppock Staeheli (New York: Simon & Schuster, Inc., 2003). Understanding how easily friendships can slide down the "slippery slope" to infatuation can help couples prevent affairs and to recover if they do occur. Maintaining "windows" within the marital relationship and "walls" with those who could threaten the marriage is the first of seven tips by the author, who also provides insight into infidelity's traumatic effects and the steps necessary for recovery.

Rekindling Desire: A Step-by-Step Program to Help Low-Sex and No-Sex Marriages, by Barry and Emily McCarthy (New York: Burnner and Routledge, 2003). Inhibited sexual desire and discrepancies in sexual desire damage marital intimacy and can drain joy from a marriage. The authors provide information for understanding and strategies for addressing these issues.

"Shedding Light on Domestic Violence," by Jane P. Ives, *www.gbod.org/marriage*. Web article formatted for download and distribution.

Stop Walking on Eggshells: Taking Back Your Life When Someone You Care About Has Borderline Personality Disorder, by Paul T. Mason, M.S. and Randi Kreger (Oakland, CA: New Harbinger Publications, Inc., 2010). The authors explore the emo-

tionally abusive and controlling behaviors of persons with low self-esteem and fear of failure, as well as the impact of those behaviors on spouses, children, and others. This supportive guide shows readers how to make sense of their situations, take back control of their lives, heal their wounds, and protect themselves and others from further damage.

Successful Second Marriages, by Patricia Bubash, M.ED. (Morgan Hill, CA: Bookstand Publishing, 2008). The author shares stories of couples in second marriages, describing how they have built happy, healthy relationships, in spite of the statistical odds against second marriages.

The Divorce Remedy: The Proven 7-Step Program for Saving Your Marriage, by Michele Weiner Davis (New York: Simon & Schuster, 2001). Written in a straightforward, personal manner, this book offers clear steps, encouragement, and hope for persons on the brink of divorce. The author lays out strategies that can be implemented by one partner in the marriage, even if the other shows no interest in working on the relationship. Focusing on one's self and taking responsibility for one's own attitudes and behavior help one feel better about one's self, regardless of the outcome for the relationship. Even happily married couples might learn from this book some ways to fine-tune their relationships!

"When a Spouse Has Suffered From Childhood Sexual Abuse," by Jane P. Ives, *www.gbod.org/marriage*. Web article formatted for download and distribution.

You Don't Have to Take It Anymore: Turn Your Resentful, Angry, or Emotionally Abusive Relationship Into a Compassionate, Loving One, by Steven Stosny, PhD (New York, NY: Simon & Schuster, Inc., 2006). The author, acclaimed for his CompassionPower program for verbally and emotionally abusive persons and their families, provides information for understanding the dynamics and impact of such abuse and for taking action to change and heal the relationships and persons involved. This text, an excellent resource for individuals, couples, and small groups, provides instruction for healing the wounds from emotional abuse, for regulating feelings so as to avoid abusive words and behavior, for reconnecting in a relationship, or for determining that a relationship is beyond repair. Visit www.compassionpower.com to learn more about the CompassionPower program and find related articles and schedules of upcoming events.

Curriculum Materials and Other Resources for Ministries With Families in Special Situations, Transitions, and Crisis

A New Beginning, an intensive three-day workshop for couples in deep distress. Contact Joshua Persall, Ministry Consultant, Family Dynamics Institute, 615-627-0751, *jpersall@familydynamics.net*, *www.familydynamics.net*.

Choosing Wisely: Before You Divorce Church Initiative, P.O. Box 1739, Wake Forest, NC 27588-1739, 800-489-7778, *Churchmail1@aol.com*, *www.divorcecare.org*. This marriage crisis counseling resource, with videos, participant workbooks, and a facilitator's guide, helps couples considering separation or divorce reconsider their decision and hopefully redirect their efforts toward restoring their marriage. By showing the spiritual, physical, emotional, and financial impact of divorce on families and on children in particular, this program attempts to stop the rapid momentum that develops when a couple begins to consider divorce and encourages them to seek help with their issues.

Developing a Successful Stepfamily Ministry, by Dick Dunn (Seagrove Beach, Florida: Singles and Stepfamily Ministries, 1995). This workbook, designed to help churches start and carry out an effective ministry of practical support for blended families, includes a cassette tape and a copy of Dick Dunn's book, *Willing to Try Again: Steps Toward Blending a Family*. The manual leads a planning team of stepfamily couples step by step through a six-session process for developing a stepfamily ministry. Available at *www.marriagesavers.org*, click on Store.

Domestic Violence: What Churches Can Do, FaithTrust Institute, 2400 N 45th St., Suite 101, Seattle, WA 98103, *www.faithtrustinstitute.org*, 206-634-1903, ext. 23, 877-860-2255. This 20-minute video provides an overview of the reality of domestic violence and raises awareness of its prevalence, dynamics, and the attitudes that underlie both abusive behavior and the fear of leaving an abusive relationship. The accompanying study guide suggests approaches for helping persons caught in such relationships and steps for congregations to take in order to minister more effectively with such families. "Safety for the woman and her children has to be addressed first. After that has been ensured, ongoing support can best be accomplished by helping the victim find appropriate community resources and providing the support of her faith community as she starts the journey of healing and decision-making for the future. The most helpful support that the congregation can offer to the abuser is to hold him accountable, to support him in taking responsibility for his behavior and recognizing that he has a problem, and to stand by him as he seeks treatment from a specialized batterers' counseling program" (Study Guide, pp. 19-20).

Marriage 911: First Response, by Joe and Michelle Williams and the National Institute of Marriage (2007), *joeandmichelle@marriage911.com*, *www.marriage911online.com*. This Christ-centered program provides resources helpful for persons in crisis marriages—whether or not the person's spouse is willing to work on healing the relationship. The *Marriage 911* 12-week Workbook provides clear steps for individuals to follow while working with an accountability partner, who uses the Support Partner Handbook. The exercises help persons shift their focus from their crisis to Christ and learn new ways of expressing their emotions. The *Marriage 911* First Aid Kit includes the workbook, handbook, DVDs for use by individuals or by leaders for a 13-week class, and a copy of Joe and Michelle's book Yes, Your Marriage Can Be Saved (Carol Stream, IL: Focus on the Family/Tyndale House, 2007). Leaders will come to your church for a weekend to help set up your Marriage 911 Ministry, asking only for travel expenses, a love offering, and opportunity to sell their books.

Retrouvaille: A Lifeline for Troubled Marriages. This Christian peer ministry begins with a weekend retreat in which husbands and wives are helped to re-establish communication and gain new understanding of themselves and each other. The presenting couples, who have experienced their own crises, share their stories of pain, reconciliation, and healing. Participants are not asked to share publicly in this setting, but learn tools and receive encouragement to rediscover each other and rebuild their relationship. Follow-up sessions provide continuing support. Couples who have experienced healing through Retrouvaille could, with training, serve as mentors for other couples in crisis. Call 1-800-470-2230 or visit *www.retrouvaille.org* for schedules and location of retreats.

Smart Stepfamilies™, *www.SmartStepfamilies.com*, founded by Ron Deal, LMFT, to help stepfamilies move toward healthy living and equip churches to minister to their unique needs. Visit this website for articles, a free e-newsletter, online webinars, book reviews, curriculum materials (*Remarriage Success, The Smart Stepfamily*), couple checkup, and conference information.

The Beyond Affairs Network (BAN) Canada: 604-859-9393; USA: 727-935-4812, *http://www.beyondaffairs.com/Seminars/*. Resources and support for those in marriages affected by infidelity, many developed by the authors of *My Husband's Affair Became the Best Thing That Ever Happened to Me*, by Anne Bercht, with Brian Bercht and Danielle Bercht (Victoria, B.C., Canada: Trafford Publishing, 2004).

The National Stepfamily Resource Center, 2315 Centennial Mall South, Suite 212, Lincoln, NE 68508, 800-735-0329, *www.stepfam.org*. This national nonprofit organization offers resources and valuable information for step-families.

The Third Option (Syracuse, NY: Family Life Education, Roman Catholic Diocese of Syracuse, 2005). 85 Fay Road, Syracuse, NY 13219. Contact Pat Ennis at (315) 472-6728 or *pat@thethirdoption.com*, or visit *www.thethirdoption.com*. This on-going program of peer ministry and relationship education combines three dynamics: a support group, "sharing" couples, and workshops on relationship skills. The first hour of the weekly (or bi-weekly) meeting offers orientation for newcomers and support group sharing for those already in the program. The second hour offers a 30-minute workshop on one of fourteen topics, which continually recycle so that participants can come in at any time. The Third Option Manual, which contains the complete program and all needed materials, is sold only to nonprofit organizations willing to offer this program free to the public. A staff person or volunteer with organizational, leadership, and relationship skills could establish and run this program in about six hours a week for the first year, three hours a week thereafter. A professional counselor should be available for occasional screening of "sharing couples" and consultation as needed. The program comes in three versions: Christian, Catholic, and secular, and although the manual is in English, Spanish worksheets and brochures make it possible for a bilingual leader to offer the program in Spanish.

Sources Cited

Amato, Paul R. and Alan Booth. 1997. *A Generation at Risk: Growing Up in an Era of Family Upheaval.* Cambridge, MA: Harvard University Press.

Arp, David and Claudia Arp. 1996. *The Second Half of Marriage.* Grand Rapids, MI: Zondervan.

Anderson, Herbert, 1998. "Marital Preparation—Protestant Perspective," *The Family Handbook*, eds. Herbert Anderson, Don Browning, Ian S. Evison, Mary Stewart Van Leeuwen. Louisville, KY: Westminster John Knox.

Augsburger, David. 1988. *Sustaining Love: Healing and Growth in the Passages of Marriage*, Ventura, CA: Regal Books.

Browning, Don S., Bonnie J. Miller-McLemore, Pamela D. Couture, K. Brynolf Lyon, Robert M. Franklin. 1997. *From Culture Wars to Common Ground: Religion and the American Family Debate.* Louisville, KY: Westminster John Knox.

Doherty, William J. "How Therapy Can Be Hazardous to Your Marital Health," presentation at Coalition for Marriage, Family, and Couples Education (CMFCE) conference, Washington, DC, July 3, 1999.

Duvall, Evelyn Millis. 1977. *Marriage and Family Development.* Philadelphia: J.B. Lippincott Co.

Ebinger, Warren and Mary Ebinger. 1998. *Do-It-Yourself Marriage Enrichment: A Workshop on Your Own Time, on Your Own Terms, on Your Own Turf.* Nashville, TN: Abingdon Press.

First United Methodist Church Wedding Guidelines and Procedures. 1977. Buchannon, WV: First United Methodist Church.

Fortune, Marie M. 1987. *Keeping the Faith: Questions and Answers for the Abused Woman.* San Francisco: Harper & Row.

Friedman, Edwin H. 1985. *Generation to Generation: Family Process in Church and Synagogue.* New York: Guilford Press.

Gray, John. 1994. *What Your Mother Couldn't Tell You and Your Father Didn't Know: Advanced Relationship Skills for Better Communication and Lasting Intimacy*. New York: HarperCollins.

Gottman, John, with Nan Silver. 1994. *Why Marriages Succeed or Fail*. New York: Simon & Schuster.

Harley, Willard F. Jr. 1994. *His Needs, Her Needs: Building An Affair-Proof Marriage*. Grand Rapids, MI: Fleming H. Revell.

Hendrix, Harville. 1988. *Getting the Love You Want*. New York: Harper & Row.

Horn, Wade. 2000. "Use Welfare Money to Promote Marriage." Coalition for Marriage, Family and Couples Education, April 4.

Hunt, Richard and Joan Hunt. 1996. *Caring Couples Network Handbook*. Nashville, TN: Discipleship Resources.

Is Your Marriage Tearing You Apart? Brochure for Retrouvaille: A Lifeline for Troubled Marriages.

Jarrell, Anne. 2000. "Puppy Lust: The Face of Sex Grows Younger and Younger." *Sunday Gazette-Mail*, Charleston, WV, April 16.

Johnson, Robert A. 1974. *He: Understanding Masculine Psychology*. King of Prussia, PA: Religious Publishing Company.

_____, 1976. *She: Understanding Feminine Psychology*. King of Prussia, PA: Religious Publishing Company.

_____, 1983. *We: Understanding the Psychology of Romantic Love*. San Francisco: Harper & Row.

Lowe, Dennis, Emily Scott-Lowe, and Sara Jackson. 1998. "Marriage Mentors: Experienced Guides Who Help Couples Navigate the Journey of Marriage" paper for Coalition for Marriage, Family, and Couples Education, Center for the Family, Pepperdine University, Malibu, CA, July 11.

Mace, David R. 1982. *Close Companions: The Marriage Enrichment Handbook*. New York: Continuum.

_____, and Vera Mace. 1997. *How to Have a Happy Marriage: A Step-by-Step Guide to an Enriched Relationship*. Nashville, TN: Abingdon Press.

Marriage Preparation in the Catholic Church: Getting It Right. 1995. Omaha, NE: Center for Marriage and Family, Creighton University.

McManus, Michael J. 1999. *A Manual on How to Create a Marriage Savers Congregation*. Bethesda, MD: Marriage Savers, Inc.

_____, 1995. *Marriage Savers: Helping Your Friends and Family Avoid Divorce*. Grand Rapids, MI: Zondervan.

Miles, Al. 2000. *Domestic Violence: What Every Pastor Needs to Know*. Minneapolis, MN: Fortress.

Ministry to Interchurch Marriages: A National Study. 1999. Omaha, NE: Center for Marriage and Family, Creighton University.

Miller, Sherod, Phyllis Miller, Elam W. Nunnally, Daniel B. Wackman, 1991. *Talking and Listening Together: Couple Communication I.* Littleton, CO: Interpersonal Communication Programs, Inc.

Nichols, William C. 1988. *Marital Therapy: An Integrative Approach.* New York: Guilford Press.

Parker, Kathleen. 1999. *Happy Marriage-Oxymoron.* Syndicated column, July 15.

Pittman, Frank. 1998. *Grow Up! How Taking Responsibility Can Make You a Happy Adult.* New York: Golden Books.

Popenoe, David and Barbara Dafoe Whitehead. 1999. *The State of Our Unions: The Social Health of Marriage in America.* New Brunswick, NJ: The National Marriage Project, Rutgers University, June.

Stanley, Scott. 1999. *Coalition for Marriage, Family, and Couples Education,* LLC (CMFCE).

Sollee, Diane. 1996. "Shifting Gears: An Optimistic View of the Future of Marriage," presented at Communitarian Pro-Family Policies, Washington, DC, November 15.

Tannen, Deborah. 1990. *You Just Don't Understand: Women and Men in Conversation.* New York: Ballentine Books.

The Book of Discipline of The United Methodist Church, 2012. Nashville, TN: The United Methodist Publishing House.

The United Methodist Hymnal; The United Methodist Book of Worship. 1989. Nashville, TN: The United Methodist Publishing House.

Waite, Linda J. 1995. "Does Marriage Matter?" *Demography,* Vol. 32, No. 4, November, pp. 483-507.

Wallace, Catherine M. 1998. *For Fidelity: How Intimacy and Commitment Enrich Our Lives.* New York: Alfred A. Knopf.

Wallerstein, Judith S. and Sandra Balkeslee. 1998. *Second Chances: Men, Women, and Children a Decade After Divorce.* New York: Ticknor & Fields.

Worthington, Everett L. Jr. 1989. *Marriage Counseling: A Christian Approach to Counseling Couples.* Downers Grove, IL: InterVarsity.

Zwack, Joseph P. 1987. *Premarital Agreements: When, Why, and How to Write Them.* New York: Harper & Row.

MARRIAGE PREPARATION

EVALUATION FORM

(Make 2 copies for each couple.)

Your feedback on our marriage preparation offerings can help us strengthen and improve our program. Although your particular responses will be kept confidential, information from these evaluations will be included in general summary reports. We suggest that husband and wife complete these forms independently first, then discuss, adding to the forms any new insights that surface during your sharing. Please return to pastor by _____.

Name _____

Date of Wedding _____   Date of Evaluation Responses _____

   Please rate each of the following on a scale of 1 (least helpful) to 5 (most helpful). Mark NA (Not Applicable) for any in which you did not participate. On the back of this form, please comment on anything that was particularly helpful or that could be improved.

<u>**Least–Most**</u>

Premarital counseling with the pastor   **NA 1 2 3 4 5**

Post-marital counseling with the pastor   **NA 1 2 3 4 5**

GROWING LOVE IN CHRISTIAN MARRIAGE Couple's Manual   **NA 1 2 3 4 5**
   Check all that describe how used:
   ____ With the pastor   ____With mentor couple   ____ In group sessions   ____ Privately as a couple

Use of a premarital inventory   **NA 1 2 3 4 5**
   Name of inventory used:

Mentoring by a married couple   **NA 1 2 3 4 5**
   Name of inventory used:

Group activities   **NA 1 2 3 4 5**
   Name of inventory used:

   Name/description

Counseling and/or consultation with other professional(s)   **NA 1 2 3 4 5**
   Name of inventory used:

   Name/description

Other resource materials or activities: **NA 1 2 3 4 5**
   Name/description

To what extent have you felt prepared and equipped for building a lasting, healthy marriage?

What needs do you have now or anticipate in the future? Use back of form as needed.